How to Kill a Princess

-And find true love

"A servant girl offers herself to her king because she fears him and needs him to survive, a queen offers herself to her king because she loves him and considers him her equal."

"Never mistake me for a servant." –Angela DeVere

The first step towards killing off your inner princess and finding a healthier path towards a truly happy ending is to retrain your heart and mind to think like a queen.

By the time you finish reading this book and apply its 5 tests to your man, you will not have to wonder who the frogs are, you will already know.

This book is *not* for men, *or their* intentions. It is for a woman's quite frankly, yours and mine.

So stop waiting for Prince Charming to friend request you someday on your Facebook page, and step away from your hopes of once upon a time, it's time to take matters into your own hands.

For Blake and Hannah

My true loves...

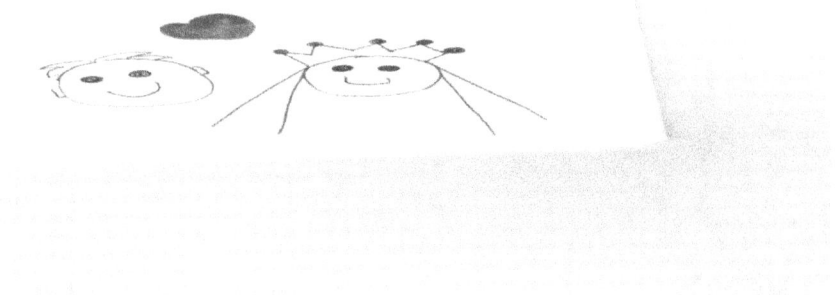

CONTENTS

Chapter 1 Decisions
The laws of attraction & human chemistry
Family past
Astrological Compatibility
Chapter 1 Test

Chapter 2 Chivalry and Truth
When Boys act like Boys
Calling them out on BS
Examples: Stories, Body Language
Chivalry Before and After Sex
Chapter 2 Test

Chapter 3 Sharing
The 1 Hr Sexual "Torture" Test
The explicit1 hr sexual torture test most men will fail
Can they handle sharing the power, and taking direction?
Guarding your heart, do not confuse sex with intimacy or love.
Chapter 3 Test

Chapter 4 Real Potential
Can he be there for you when you really need him?
Kids and Relationships
Family and Friends
Co-Dependency vs. Interdependent
Generations
Chapter 4 Test

Chapter 5 Commitment
The Big Fight
Forgiveness Factor
Letting them Go
Commitment is a Choice
What is Love?
Chapter 5 Test
Final Exam
Closing

Introduction

I feel I must disclose in my introduction that I am not a typical disillusioned woman looking for my superman. Hopefully, because you were smart enough to pick up this book, neither are you. I was that doe eyed girl, the teenage bride waiting for magical fairy dust to carry me away into matrimonial bliss, and then quite stubbornly I woke up.

This book is a journey of information and solicited, unfiltered advice on how to find your diamond in the rough. The diamond that I personally seek lies deep beneath the romantic fluff and glittering lights of Hollywood heroines and fairy tale endings. I am not looking for a prince to save me, or a meek masculine mind to control. I simply seek my equal; A man who is my best friend.

My wise cracking great grandmother used to say. "Men always want what they can't have, and when they finally get it they don't want it anymore." –

She also said, "Men never grow up… they just get taller." –
-I'm pretty sure she was a genius.

This is my story about truly equal intentional love, and the 5 tests I created to find it.

We as kind, intelligent, female nurturers know how to take care of our men. I mean we sprouted from the Disney princess generation and grew up watching Cosby on TV; so we totally have a handle on what to do when our kids don't eat their vegetables, or when we find a cigarette in little Johnny's backpack right?

Yet as modern American women proudly juggling our own version of prime time variety shows, we still seek tangible equality in the workplace and in the home. The distant aspiration of an equal partnership that is love, duty, honor and laundry.

However, because most of us have learned at a very young age that taking care of *most* men is much easier than cleaning up after they "tidy" for us, we tend to make excuses for their boyish behavior; treat grown men like our own offspring, and now have successfully raised a society of very tall male babies. "Winning" a boyfriend or husband by "acting" like the type of woman you think he desires, is just as immature as keeping an adorable dolphin in your bathtub. "It is in the selfish act of keeping itself, that breeds contempt."

Because most American men have been spoon fed so much tolerance by starry eyed romantically obsessed girls and their own moms, they are now able to get away with just about anything. You know what I mean, many men have a tendency to half ass household chores, relationships and child rearing because they have been enabled to. Why? because they *know* you will pick up the slack. They have been trained to realize that whatever they don't finish when a woman is present, she will come behind him and finish it; if for no other reason than because it often drives her crazy to see things half done. For example, did he wipe off the counter and appliances and sweep the floor when he "cleaned" the kitchen? Or just unload the dishwasher? Thought so… How many men do you know that live alone and have a clean house *without* the use of a girlfriend, family member or a maid assisting them? Are the top priorities of most of the men that you know their families or girlfriend's happiness and well being, or with how many new apps they can buy for their latest phone? It seems that we have not only taken a back seat to the new technologies in our society, but that we are also left cleaning up the messes that a lack of honest face to face daily communication can bring. I am not blindly claiming that emotionally mature, self capable men do not exist, but that they are few and far between, and that we have collectively become part of the problem that they are so rare.

So, we cook for them, clean for them, give them sex, buy them video game players, wash their clothes, and offer unsolicited advice when they misbehave or treat us badly. We often giggle when their selfish, cruel or immature behavior makes them "one of the guys."

Is it really charming and adorable when he ogles the women at Hooters and plays Wii with his buddy until 2 am; or do you find yourself hanging out in the bedroom asking your mom on line two where all the men went? Praising him as if he had just won the Nobel Peace Prize for simply taking out the trash is the same as giving your child a cookie for only doing 3 sentences of homework. Ladies, unless you have no children and no job and you feel your only calling in life is to wait on a man hand and foot, then what the hell chica? We women have slowly created a male counterpart monster, and then we have the audacity to wonder what their intentions with us truly are. Things that make ya go Hmmm?...

We must learn to retrain our own minds and expectations of relationships before we try to seek out and destroy what most of us have enabled in men for years. This of course does not apply to all men, there are a few good ones left who do not seek to merely play with your body and/or your mind. A few of them actually want to love someone in this lifetime and to be loved in return. If you are ready to find him, let's begin...

This book contains lessons, a few quizzes, true stories and some of my personal experiences. Each of the five chapters are actually tests that you can apply to your relationships. The following are your first 5 mini lessons, please reread as necessary.

Mini Lesson 1
Lifespan reality check

Do not waste anymore of your time serial dating for 6-12 months at a time before you realize someone is no good for you. It is a lesson I learned to nip losers in the bud quickly, and I highly recommend you do the same. Life is too short.

Mini Lesson 2
Love yourself

You cannot be happy *in* a relationship unless *you* are happy. This is a very simple statement, but very true. It is so important to be comfortable in your own skin, with the person you are when you are alone and "non-hitched" before you can truly learn how to be happy with someone else. You are not being bitchy or evil or selfish to desire a man who acts like a man, start retraining your mind from being the damsel in distress or the stoic martyr. Figure out what makes you truly happy. Love yourself enough to desire the kind of love you deserve.

Mini Lesson 3
What does he want from me?

It is illogical for us to ask a man when we first meet him what his intentions with us are. How can he know what he wants from you, until he knows you? And believe me; he won't feel he knows you until you have had some time for innuendo, foreplay or sex, at least one good fight, and a few bad trips through your menstrual cycle.

After a few casual dates if you feel he can handle the next tests, you can decide how far to take your intimacy level and may choose to offer him small doses of your female mood swing reality.

Do not let his behavior towards you define what you become in the relationship. Become what you want in the relationship, he can either fit or you can yell…Next! However, in order to investigate any potential suitor properly you need to follow the five tests in an orderly manner and then sit back to study the results. In most cases it will become apparent after only a few dates if he can even make past test number two. Remind yourself constantly that it is not your job in life to make him happy, you are not his mom. His mom may be part of his problem.

Mini Lesson 4

You're Intentions

What you intend to get out of a relationship is what you will ultimately get, whether you realize it or not. Are you attracted consistently to people that you believe you can change? Everyone loves the bad boy at some point in their lives, and not all bad boys are bad, they are usually just too immature to see the errors of their ways. We will be taking a closer look in the following chapters at the laws of attraction to find out why we are sometimes naïve glutens for punishment.

Mini Lesson 5

It's all you

Everyone is attracted to different things, and for very different reasons. The first step is to really consider what you want from a man and why you want it. First, look at yourself and your wants and needs in a very non-judgemental way. I'm not here to tell you exactly what kind of man you should seek. That is a very personal decision based on your own requirements. We will examine the laws of attraction and compatibility, but the choice is ultimately yours alone.

This book is designed to give you the tools needed to see if the men you pick will be able to measure up to your expectations. If they do not, it will be very easy for you to see, and you can move on without wasting too much time or heartache in the process.

It is my greatest hope, my fellow former princesses, to help you find out what makes *you* really tick before you go back out and settle for whoever else may come along. You may disagree with some of my methods and ideals if you cannot keep an open mind, but I assure you there is always a reason to my rhyme. If my past mistakes before my awakening were any indication of life's learning lessons about who not to date, I'm pretty sure I have earned a PhD from somewhere.

.

Chapter 1

Decisions & the Laws of Attraction

Ok ladies; …Are you ready to go love shopping?

It is always a good idea to do your research before you undertake any new venture. This should be especially true if your venture includes another human being.

This book is full of facts, biased opinions, tests, tips and what I hope is recognized as humor, but please remind yourself at every possible chance you can; that you are a human being with wants, needs and desires and so is he, (or they) depending on how much you intend to take on. Enclosed are the tools designed to help me *and you* find the ones we are looking for. And heads up ladies, it better not be the same guy. I'm a sexy published author, soo good luck with that. ;)

Take a few moments and think about your past relationships, how did they begin? How did they end? Why did they end? You may be reminded right now of something he did or didn't do, and you wish he would have done differently, and everything would be fine right now, and you wouldn't have to be reading this stupid book because you'd be married or at least living together, and enjoying happily ever after right?

The fact that he so obviously messed up the relationship and doesn't have you in his life anymore, is punishment enough for him right now… You're welcome…

The fact that he wasn't ready to take on the type of commitment that you were so desperately hoping for with him makes him an ignorant fool right? Well, maybe yes, maybe no, maybe it's a giant blessing in disguise, maybe it was bad timing, maybe you were too aggressive or too shy and didn't follow the five tests in this book, or maybe it just wasn't meant to be. Move on, you don't need an ignorant fool hanging around anyway. If you think about whatever it is he did to lose you in the first place, I'm sure you will come to the conclusion *again* that he wasn't worth it anyway. His mistakes are actually irrelevant; it is how you handled his mistakes that make all the difference in the world.

"Sometimes, it takes an asshole to shake us out of the toilet and remind us of who we are and who we really want to share our bathrooms with." So let's take a moment to truly thank the old assholes. We can now examine our past and future relationships, and learn from our mistakes, together.

Timing, as they say can be everything. When was your last relationship? Chances are if you just broke up last Tuesday, you are not ready to go love shopping quite yet. If that is the case, first read this book once or twice, do some soul searching, spend time with family and friends; meditate on what you want from your relationships and in a month or two depending on your personal situation, you should be ready to start looking again. If you were really crushed or became too attached to your last partner, you may want to consider some counseling to get yourself back in the right frame of mind before dating again. Remember, we must first be happy alone before we can be truly happy with someone else.

{ READ 10 TIMES }

Another human being should never define you. If you feel like you always have to be in a relationship even if it's bad, it's time for you to do some serious soul searching. You need to find out which parts of yourself you feel you are lacking, and why, so that you aren't trying to fill in the gaps with someone else's personality.

Our society acts as if women need to pair up with a man like we are boarding Noah's ark before a mass extinction. Take your time to look for Mr. Right, you don't need to settle for a swaggering lion if you really want a panda bear.

Our partners should always be a compliment to our lives and walk beside us, they are not there to fill us up, or tear us down. Yes, have healthy amounts of love, understanding and empathy in your heart towards your man, but do not be a doormat.

Some of you are quite frankly, looking for marriage, others are not. Take a step back to see how much freedom it is that you desire.

If your last break up was a little farther in the past, like last Wednesday for instance, let's take a look at how your current lifestyle can contribute to your relationships success or its possible demise. What do you do for a living? What type of hours do you work?

Unless you have won the lottery or are lucky enough to be a trust fund baby, you probably have a job. Even if you have been a stay at home mom, (which we all know is one of the most challenging careers). You have a life.

Does a meaningful relationship fit into your life right now? If you don't want a serious relationship, do you have at least a few hours a week to devote to just getting to know someone? Decide from the very beginning how much you are willing to give, of your time, and of yourself to each person that you decide to date. After a few dates if you're hitting it off, make it clear to the other person that you have a busy schedule, but you will try to make time at least once a week to get together.

It is a good idea, if you can, to pick a day that is "your day". For example, if you know you are usually free on Saturday's at seven p.m. and so is he, try and schedule that time for each other, even if it's just to grab a coffee.

Nothing is more frustrating than flaky vagueness. If your days off work or school etc. alternate; agreeing to a date once or twice a month is fine. You do not need to see him and call him every day, just some sort of a basic understanding between your schedules is necessary so that neither party is confused about what is expected from the other. Not knowing what his or *your own* schedule expectations are is unacceptable. It is a complete waste of *your* time. If you are not sure enough that you want to see him at least once a month move on right away, or don't start anything with him at all.

When you find you are ready to take the plunge and begin looking for Mr. Right again, there are some interesting things to learn about basic compatibility. Read through them very carefully before you go out on your next date. If you feel he is only arranging times in his life for you ohh say,…after 10 p.m. for instance, call him out on the booty call no no, and cut him off completely.

"Sometimes what appears to be a diamond in the rough can be just be his charming smile blinding you. You need to look close enough to see if 666 is tattooed somewhere on the back of his head."
Gracias E.W.

The first poem I ever remember writing was in the 4th grade about a little boy in my music class.
Little did I know this poem would set the tone for what was to be my love life for the next 20 years.

My heart of glass is easily broken, whenever harsh words are heard or spoken, I've tried scotch tape and super glue; but my heart says all it needs is you.

-Moi at age 11

Turns out, all I really needed at age 11 in 1984 was an Atari, to level my playing field with all the neighborhood boys..

Good job Santa,..I got an easy bake oven

The Laws of Attraction

Let's face it ladies, do you wanna have sex with him? If you have to look very long or hard at someone before you find something you like chances are your physical compatibility will fizzle out very quickly. Does he take your breath away, with a look? Do you find yourself fantasizing about the two of you in bed? God knows he does, if he has noticed you...

Women are all attracted to different things when we first meet a man. I personally happen to look to see if his eyes have power, humor and intelligence, and of course his chest and ass. Where else can a queen lay her head but a nice chest and ass?

Many women I have asked said they look for his eye color, his hair, his smile, his arms, his height and his weight. We all have an idea in our minds of what our ideal mate should look like. Some women prefer the tall blond surfer, some the shorter stockier teddy bear. The question is **why** do we look for those things? What is it that forms our individual opinions on what is attractive and what is not?

Basic Male and Female Chemistry 101

There have been many great studies and theories about what causes human attraction. However, a great deal of research and testing has been done recently into the why and how of what we desire and the simple magic of human chemistry. Much of the research suggests that some attractions differ significantly by gender; and that we are somehow vying for perfection by looking for our idea of our ideal selves. More recently the discovery of human pheromones, nature's magnetic wonder has led some to believe we are not that much removed from our animal counterparts in what steers us to our sexual partners.

A clinical researcher named Scott Gustafon tested a hypothesis in 1989. His theory was that humans are drawn to those most like our ideal picture of ourselves. In other words, an ideal mates features and body language would mimic our own, *or* be opposite if we feel our ideal self is not adequate in some way. It seems that according to this study that birds of a feather really do flock together, and yes Paula...opposites attract.

It has also been closely observed that men and women are both attracted, even if subconsciously, to those they feel would give their offspring the greatest advantage. Men love an hourglass figure and womanly body, not too skinny or too fat, but curvaceous and healthy. Other attraction getters at the top of his list: a great smile, a happy temperament, sense of humor, and energetic feminine eyes. Woman who are healthy are more likely to conceive healthy, well balanced attractive children. This is a basic instinct men follow even if they are not looking to start a family. This stereotypical attraction by men is shared in almost all cultures around the world. (Traflinger 1996, Norman 1998)

Men tend to rate physical qualities above all else, whereas women rate stability and security for her brood at the top. Human evolution has taught the hunter gatherer societies to each look for what would make the human race most successful. A muscular, tall athletic man is most women's ideal body type. It is thought that because of his strength and size, our instincts tell us that he would be a good hunter, be able to provide food for his family, and protection for us against other males.

Speaking of size, most women prefer a man to be at least her height when she is wearing heels, it is simply a matter of physical compatibility. Otherwise he is probably too short to make her feel protected (And to wear heels beside him) ☺ In evolutions defense, if both genders were looking for the same height at the same time there would be a lot less chance of human procreation for many people..

Love stinks? It is now widely believed that human pheromones signal an invisible mating call of sorts. Pheromones act much like hormones but they are released by one person and can cause physiological and behavior changes in another. Most scientists believe pheromones are detected through the nasal passages or the VNO the volmeronasal organ; a pair of tiny pits in the nose.

A 2002 study led by Evolutionary biologist Randy Thornhill from The University of New Mexico found that women prefer the scent of a man *somewhat* similar to their own over the scent of nearly genetically identical or totally dissimilar men. It seems symmetry in body composition and facial structure tells a potential mate that you have evolved to a higher place in the gene pool or are not too closely related to mate.

Borrowing sweaty undershirts from a variety of men, Thornhill offered the shirts for women to smell, without seeing the men in person but only asking them what their impressions of the scents were. Without a doubt, the women found the scent of a more symmetrical man to be more attractive and desirable, even though they couldn't see them! This was especially true if the woman was menstruating. Pheromones can affect our attractions it seems even subconsciously. In some cases women in Thornhills study reported not smelling anything at all on a shirt, but still found themselves mysteriously attracted to it.

Scientists have also discovered that scent plays an important role in deeming females attractive. Two putative pheromones which are released at different rates during the menstrual cycle can stimulate the blood flow to the hypothalamus in men's brains, but not in women. It seems nature signals silently these timely moments to men but why?

Women have been programmed to be more discerning because we only produce about 400 eggs in our lifetime, whereas men produce sperm by the thousands. Because pregnancy and child rearing can take such a toll on women, our preferences are based more on security and longevity vs. attractiveness alone. For men it is almost as if they are notified by scent when we are in heat, or when we are experiencing ovulation.

Misery loves Company? It has long been recognized that women who work closely or live together for any length of time will develop a similar menstrual cycle. This is believed to be caused by a pheromone in women's underarm sweat and has been documented since the 1970's. This theory is called the McClintock effect.

Many recent studies suggest that a male's scent and pheromones play an intragal part in maintaining the reproductive health of women. Researchers at the Monell Chemical Senses Center and The University of Pennsylvania School of Medicine found that women who have sex with a man at least once a week are more likely to have normal menstrual cycles, fewer infertility problems, and milder menopause than women who were either celibate or only having sex sporadically. Because it seems pheromones can play such a huge part on human physiological sexual attraction and behavior; it may be wise to lay off so much heavy deodorant and perfumes and just let your noses do the walking.

In chapter two we will take an in depth look at body language and communication as an indication of true or playerized interest; but a good indication of his attraction to you is his eye contact and gestures. A man who is tuned into you will have his whole body facing you during conversation. He may lean in and look directly into your eyes as he is speaking. If he is tapping his finger or keeps checking the time he is probably bored or may have another woman waiting for him elsewhere. If he strokes his chin often, it means he is passing judgment.

Works Cited
3. Norman, Jan. – The Evolutionary Theory of Attraction" The Human Sexuality Web 21 April 1998. 8 Oct. 2001.
4. Traflinger, Richard F. –Reproduction and Society" Social Basis of Human Sexual Attraction

  1. The evolutionary Theory of Sexual Attraction, a site posted by the University of Missouri, Kansas City.

2. Buss. The Evolution of Desire: Strategies of Human Mating. New York: HarperCollins, 1994.
3. Brain Scans Reveal Human Pheromones, a news source found by encyclopedia brittanica when entered the search key word, "sexual attraction"

Overheard at the water cooler:

Can you somehow be de-magnetized for attracting losers and drama or is that something you can only buy jerk repellant for?

Family History and Psychological Basis for Human Mating

Society has told us for generations that we marry our parents. If that is true and so many people say things like "I am never going to turn into my mother or father.", then why do we do it? It may be simpler than you think. If you feel subconsciously that one of your parents was not doing a good job of either keeping their relationship together or that they handled many situations in your childhood wrong, you may try to seek out that flawed parents personality in your mate selection so that you can change them. Yep,.. I said the c word.

Was one of your parents a control freak, alcoholic, abusive, to meek, too aggressive, the martyr, too stuffy, too immature? Have you found yourself drawn to those types of people without even realizing it, and then when you finally see their personality flaws you try and just "fix" them? I thought so. Usually our first dating relationships with men are the ones where we think we have found true love, and then one day we wake up and we realize we are dating our father, or uncle or grandfather etc, and nothing we have said or have done differently than our mothers or aunts or grandmothers has changed anything in him at all.

Light bulb time chicas!

These men cannot be blamed for their falling short of our expectations, the truth is, they are what they are and they expect to be loved as they are, just like you do. When we try and force someone else to fit into a mold that we created for them, chances are it will end up looking like the play-doh hair salon and you'll have fluorescent green strands of spaghetti all over the floor.

Compatibility does not mean find a man from the same side of town or from your MySpace top 8 that you can train; you must first train yourself to look for the right types of compatible traits and then filter out the green spaghetti. I am not making excuses for these men to be able to act like jerks, on the contrary. I am trying to help you understand that they exist, and it's better to steer clear of them than get yourself into a relationship with one or try and change him.

A man for instance, that had a loving mother, a sister or often a lot of early female influence in his life would learn at an young age that he can easily manipulate women because he is just so darn cute. However, as much as he loves his mother, if his real father was absent from his life either emotionally or physically he may subconsciously blame her for not being strong enough or attractive enough to keep daddy around. Even if a stepfather is eventually in the picture, his longing for his paternal ties will make him second guess what she did wrong.

If dad *was* in the picture, was dad the meek passive aggressive type that let mom run the show? This does not happen in every case, but to some men whose environment and physiology happen to be in the right place at the right time it can create the perfect breeding ground for behavioral abnormalities later in life. Why?, If he loves his mother seemingly unconditionally, but can charm her easily, he realizes she is weak and controllable. This type of man will almost always seek out his mother as a mate. A caring, motherly figure who will in some ways resemble his mom so that he can manipulate, control, protect and teach her "strength" through his selfish behavior, absence, cheating etc. He will think he has found gold, his soul mate. If his mother was a controlling overbearing type A, he may try to seek out his mom as a mate and change her into what he longed for her to really be.

He will be charming, witty and kind almost to a fault at first, and then he will expect her start handling his control issues little by little. He will suddenly be too busy for her, working, playing, cheating etc. and then still expect her to treat him like he is man of the year...

In this way, he is subconsciously teaching her and his mother a lesson. He will want her welcomed into the family or at least a friend group within a relatively short amount of time so that he can show off his new prize. This man will continue to manipulate and be very promiscuous with other women on the side as part of an ego stroking game; leaving you enough clues to question his fidelity but lying like a fox even when he's confronted with some proof.

These men are often very defensive when they are questioned on any personal behavior and will try and make you feel guilty for even suggesting that they would lie.

In his mind he thinks: see mom, I treated so and so badly this week, and she is still around. If you were as "strong" as her you might still be with my father. Or at least be a better part of his life. He will tend to look for similar body shape, ethnicity, personality, and very often a young woman or a single mom of any age that he feels is vulnerable enough to be controlled, but "strong enough" in his confused mind to not leave an emotionally abusive relationship. Sadly, very often he finds her.

It is his goal to find the woman who is "strong enough" to never leave him no matter what he may dish out. If he has been left by a woman before, his behavior will only escalate. He is looking for the girl who "understands" his selfish behavior and will essentially be more like a mother or daughter to him than an equal partner. He will do this all with one hand tied behind his back, while he is rubbing your neck and telling you how much he really cares.

The heartbreak of this story, is that this *is* the man many women will try and seek out to change and why so many women are cheated on, or emotionally and physically abused…but still stay. They stay in a codependent relationship because they don't know how to step out of the nightmare and break the cycle. More on codependency later…

If this sounds like you, I am truly sorry for what you have gone through. I was her once too. It took a long time for me to realize I would rather live in a cave with no food and water in Siberia, then to stay in that relationship for one more day. Leaving that life was the single most painful thing that I have ever done. Most of what was once me had slowly died. But finally, one breath at a time I rebuilt my life, and my hopes and my belief in myself returned. Now, I see the strength in my choice to move on and I am grateful to have my identity back.

"I wish, to not merely wish, but to plan. To not live in fear of bad decisions but to live free, and laugh when it all falls to pieces. That is a good life."

AFGHANI WOMEN

Longing for sunlight,

The shrouded minds grow.

Half rooted,

For fear of their secret garden's plight.

Their reaper beats them down,

But they will grow again;

And one day

They shall see the sun.

-A. Devere

Since we are on the topic of behavior I found an interesting checklist to help discern if someone you may know, or have had a relationship with, may actually be mentally unstable.

The man discussed in the above article is a typical sociopath. This information is recognized by most psychologists and can be found in many books as well as the internet if you choose to research it further. After you read this, you may be very surprised. I can guarantee that you have either met or possibly even dated a man with most of these characteristics. The following is from: Psychopath Checklist of H Cleckley nd R. Hare and its related qualities.

Personality Traits and Behavioral Characteristics of a Sociopath:

Glib/Superficial Charm: Can charm the pants off most anyone, warm smile appearance and hygiene, self assured, lightly cocky, easy going temperament and sense of humor, average to above average intelligence, on the surface they are magnetic and charming but they are overtly cold, domineering, and manipulative to others to get what they want.

Grandiose sense of self: Feels entitled to certain things as their/his right, speaks highly or exaggerates his achievements especially to women. Is proud of his boyish sly behavior, always looking for more ways to prop himself up in the eyes of others.

Pathological Lying: Has no problem lying while remaining calm, this personality will lie to your face without flinching, has been known to pass lie detectors tests, excels at his evasion of accountability. Rarely blinks when lying, however the eyes may twitch, his lying stare will either cut right through you as a warning, or he may choose to avoid eye contact all together if he thinks you have figured him out.
When caught in a lie, he will first deny everything and then if not believed deliver a counter attack to either feign being a victim himself or try and prove he is a changed man to those who are trained to believe him

Lack of Remorse or Guilt: Repressed rage is at the core, sees friends and lovers as either accomplices or his victims, will never offer a sincere apology for hurting someone no matter what the circumstances may be, unremorseful, bitter, often in his mind he places the blame on his victim for not being strong enough to handle him, sees most others as weak for allowing their feelings and emotions to surface, appears to care but in a feigned cold way, sees love as a way to manipulate and control, often places blame on others. No true sense of responsibility for their actions.

Shallow or Cold Emotions: When they show "warmth" or joy it is either feigned or from experience and usually serves an ulterior motive. Outraged by little things that might make them look bad or be "found out" yet remaining unmoved or cold by what would upset a normal person. Often will say things like, "I don't let anything bother me", Sees any type of emotional need or caring from others as drama or weakness, will be contemptuous of those who seek to truly understand him.

Incapacity for Real Love: Constant need for stimulation, their "love" always has stipulations and control attached, lives in the moment, cannot stand to make solid plans, flaky, shady and secretive behavior, indecisive, promiscuous with no apparent boundaries. Easily bored and always on the move, Often this personality is good with young children and can make them believe that they are father of the year with their peter pan charm. Most children will not recognize that they are being manipulated and controlled as well. Seeks out people where his behavior will be tolerated, condoned, admired

Lack of Empathy: Unable to empathize with the pain they cause, they see pain and suffering as weakness and vulnerability. Unable to recognize that there is anything wrong with them. Though outwardly he may be spiritual or even religious, he places little value on human life, or the afterlife. If someone they have hurt or manipulated calls them out on their behavior they will casually figure out a way to regain control, or end the relationship with you if they feel that you can no longer be controlled and may eventually leave him. Because of this common behavior to "cut" someone off, he will have few very close friends at a time, Incapable of real human attachment to another.

Impulsive: Wants instant gratification, has difficulty making commitments of any kind, unreliable, since they are not genuine neither are their promises, Believe they are entitled to most whims without concern for impact on others. Will have difficulty making plans, and may change his plans often at the last minute, Will go where he feels his ego can be best stroked at any given time. Only concerned about how a potential crisis will impact him personally. Changes his mind with the weather.

History of Juvenile Delinquency: Is good at conning others, problems keeping the same close friends for any length of time, possible gang activity to create a new family, history in juvenile teen years of either, stealing, cheating, vandalism, arson, cruelty or abuse. This behavior usually surfaces around age 15, they will cause havoc without any thought for safety of others, and insincere remorse if they are caught or punished, excels at evasion of accountability.

Promiscuous or Infidelity: Promiscuity, views women as playthings, is proud of his sexual prowess and exploits, indiscriminate selection of sexual partners, will have several sexual partners at the same time, is usually manipulating multiple people in secret at the same time as a sort of game or power play, no concern for sexually transmitted diseases or pregnancy. Most often if one of his playthings becomes pregnant he will either cut her off completely or regain control of her until she has an abortion or he can figure out a way to use her and the child to his advantage.

Lack of realistic Life: Tends to see himself in a higher status of society than what reality allows, feels he deserves the best because he is the best.

Criminal Versatility: Able to lie or con his way out of almost any situation, will say or do just about anything to avoid prosecution, pursues vindictive behavior against anyone who would try to discredit him or unmask his feigned sanity.

Were you surprised?

If you would like more information on this important topic please read the book "The sociopath next door" by Martha Stout PHD, it is a fascinating read.

"Being able to intelligently recognize from the beginning who we should stay away from, is just as important as being able to recognize true partner compatibility."

Astrological Compatibility, What's Your Sign?

Whatever your preconceived notions may be on Astrology and Horoscopes please keep an open mind as you read through this next section. You may be surprised at how accurate this ancient art can really be at not only describing your own personality traits but assist you in unveiling who you are most compatible with.

There are four groupings of Zodiac Signs, Fire Signs, Water Signs, Earth and Air Signs. Each person is most compatible with others of their own grouping. For example an Aries as a fire sign is most compatible with other fire signs like themselves. The Fire signs are Leo, Sagittarius and other Aries. You can be compatible with a few other signs out of your grouping, but the natural attraction or connection may be more muted and usually will not be sustainable or as passionate for a lasting relationship or a deeper understanding of your partner. Those who are outside of your grouping are usually best as good friends.

THE FIRE SIGNS

Aries:
March 21ˢᵗ-April21st.
Power Color: Red, Planet: Mars

The classic idealist, you are passionate, romantic, creative, powerful, direct, humorous, and the type of person to whom others naturally gravitate. You are a magnetic firecracker that draws people in with your natural flare. You are the natural born leader and inventor, the pioneer.

You take flirting as a type of art form and tend to be openly unfaithful unless in love. Aries are very sexual creatures, talented in sports and the arts and highly adventurous. You are both sides of the romantic coin, you want to be swept off your feet in a dramatic display of love, but you don't want to be stifled, controlled or ever played upon. Aries tend to avoid lying, as it is considered to them a waste of time and a game of immaturity. Aries are impatient for others to catch up to what they seemed to have figured out five minutes ago. Aries are cocky, clever, selfish muses that will bewitch your senses and steal your heart.

Aries are very loyal to those to whom they place their love and trust; but will anger easily when their love or trust has been betrayed. When and only when, someone finally catches an Aries attention for longer than a week, an Aries will be a loving, faithful and adventurous partner.

Most successful marriages happen later in life, which is usually a second marriage because impatient Aries tend to marry young. Aries are most compatible with Sagittarius, Leos or quite often another Aries if the two of you can stop fighting over who controls the remote.

Sagittarius,:
November 23rd-December 21st
Power Color: Light Blue, Planet: Jupiter

You have a capricious nature and unforgettably friendly character, you are independent and rebellious. Your sense of humor is a force to be reckoned with in any social situation. There seems to be so many things you want to do and so little time to find to do it in. Having numerous varied interests, you have trouble juggling your spontaneous desires with your responsibilities.

You are an excitement seeker that bores easily, and have difficulty with commitments of any kind. You love the lure of travel and adventure, and are usually optimistic with a happy temperament. You tend to be sly when it comes to romantic or sexual endeavors; you want the conquest without a real commitment. Because you are so impulsive you have a high incidence of divorce and break-ups do to your infidelity. Most do not have a strong enough will power to continue a lasting faithful relationship until later in life.

When you are able to find the rare person who understands your deepest darkest secrets, and you will finally sit still long enough to listen, you will create a passionate lasting bond. You can sometimes think more like a child than an adult and seek instant gratification without much thought to those you have left in your dust. Sagittarius are most compatible with Aries, Leos and other Sagittarius, although the chances of infidelity are doubled with other Sags.

Leo:
July 24th-August 23rd
Power Color Red/Gold: Planet: The Sun

You are the party, and the center of attention. You are independent and ambitious and are drawn to power, you tend to be vain and snobbish, but in your mind you are well worth it. You are friendly, witty and intelligent. You tend to gravitate towards those who will make you look good, because appearances to you are extremely important. It matters to you what even the neighbors may think so you are always one upping those around you, most of the time without them even knowing.

You tend to have a superiority complex, and are self centered with a bit of an insincere sense of giving. If there is not enough money or power to suit your needs, you will usually move on to someone who can offer the next best thing. You are more interested in getting or being the trophy wife, when you are young than being in real committed, deep level love.

It is not until a bit later for you that you will become a mature Leo lion and fall in love with love. When you lose your temper you are a force to be reckoned with. Because you are so aggressive you know how to turn your ideas into realities, and failure is something you don't like to even consider. Because of your need for constant approval and affection you are pushed more towards marriage than the other fire signs. Many Leos marry so that they will always have someone attentive by their side; just be careful as Leos have one of the highest divorce rate of any sign. Leos are most compatible with other Leos, Aries and Sagittarius; although with other Leos it will either be love or Hate because you both need constant adoring attention.

THE EARTH SIGNS

Virgo

August 24th-September 23rd
Power Color: Brown, Planet Mercury

You are friendly and kind, but can be intimidating to others, you value respect and loyalty. You love to plan and are a creature of habit vs. spontaneity in your daily life. You have a bureaucratic intellect that can wear a person down before it wears you out. Your rigid thinking creates a lot of anxiety for you and this tends to lead you to self indulgence of many kinds.

You tend to be very athletic and have a very good work ethic. Your narrow or small mindedness on many issues makes you argumentative and manipulative to others who do not take your side. You care what others think of you and try to coordinate your life to a more favorable public opinion.

Love and marriage to you is more of a convenience than a romantic endeavor. Dating involves too much chance, and you would rather have someone waiting patiently for you at home.

Your sharp mind and intellect can lead to feelings of superiority. You are quick to criticize others or be condescending to those who do not share your views, or that do not wish to bask in your light. You are a bearer of grudges and can be resentful with great tenacity. You are selfish and controlling with your mates, after all who knows how to run other people's lives better than you? Because of this trait, Virgo's have a very high incidence of divorce. Even long after the relationship ends, you are wondering how someone could have possibly left you.

You are continually looking for ways to improve yourself and how those around you will see you. Virgos are most compatible with Taurus, Capricorns and other Virgos as long as you give each other enough space to be yourselves.

Taurus:
April 21st-May 21st
Power Color: Green, Planet: Venus

You have the strength, stamina and courage to do anything you set your mind to. You are usually monogamous when in love, honest, and hate to be toyed with. You tend to keep your emotions to yourself to keep from being vulnerable to others.

You are the strong martyr who would rather walk with the pain and stifle it, than to admit in public you are hurting. You have deep seated security needs, and seek long term relationships. You can be very encouraging and motherly to others. You are a person of substance and stability; people lean on you as you are reliable and steadfast even in hard times.

You tend to be very jealous and possessive of those close to you and do not understand their overly emotional or flirtatious behavior. If you are betrayed or cheated on you will not cause a dramatic scene but will walk away in silence hating and punishing the person from afar.

You are excellent at holding grudges and having patience in any situation. You are pragmatic and never feel you are complete without a life partner, you are usually organized and responsible with your career and finances.

You are frugal, and realistic. Taurus's tend to love marriage, and have great lasting relationships with other Earth or Water Signs. To you constant serial dating and affairs seem frivolous and for people who are too immature and emotionally impulsive.

You shine in practical and business matters and make wonderful employees. You are most compatible with other Taurus's, Virgos, and Capricorns; although another Taurus may not move quick enough to keep you interested.

Capricorn:
December 22nd-January 20th
Power Color: Gray & Black Planet: Saturn

You are kind, responsible and loyal. You may appear cold and condescending to those who don't know you, but that's usually because you only let a few good people in at a time.

You are very goal oriented and tend to be a workaholic. In matters of love you are very emotional, although it is masked with a sense of duty and practicality.

You are faithful and responsible and have a good balance of integrity. You are goal oriented but patronizing towards yourself and others. Your ego complex falters back and forth between self depravation and self indulgence. You crave ego boosts and are impatient with those who cannot see the gift before them.

You are intolerant of selfish and cruel behavior towards others, or people who are too flighty. You most admire strength, honesty, intelligence, stability and creative accomplishments. You posses a remarkable sense of realism and are very insightful; If you are betrayed by a mate your jealousy will cause physical pain, as you disdain games and lying partners. You are best matched with someone that works as hard as you do. You would make a great administrator of any kind. You do not take promises or commitments lightly. You are most compatible with Taurus's, Virgos, and other Capricorns; although another Capricorn may seem too boring to keep you interested for long.

THE WATER SIGNS

Cancer:
June 22ⁿᵈ-July 23ʳᵈ
Power Color: Violet, Planet: The Moon

You are emotional and sentimental. You wear your moods on your sleeve, and have many desires. You are warm, nurturing, kind and creative. You tend to long for a committed relationship early in life. You are shy but affectionate with those close to you. You tend to either withdraw when you are angry, or throw a tantrum in front of perfect strangers. You hold it in until it boils over into an uncontrollable firestorm and then sulk when it's all over.
You are naturally generous and giving. You do not like to be left out, and crave emotional attention. If you feel another has told a secret about you, you are crushed and horrified. In marriage you are usually a devoted partner who expects the same in return.

You tend to fall in love with the people who are all wrong for you early in life and do not learn your lesson for a while. Because you can become emotionally attached so easily, you are prone to many heartbreaks and dramatic endings. You are possessive and jealous when it comes to your mate.

You need someone who can offer you stability and emotional security. If you go for the flirt you will crash and burn all over again. Love and devotion revitalizes your soul, you are in a sense in love with love itself. Your concern for the welfare of others makes you a great friend and social activist of any kind. You are most compatible with other Cancer's, Pisces, and Scorpio

Scorpio:
October 24th-November 22nd
Power Color: Black & Purple, Planet: Pluto and Mars

You are compassionate, kind and intuitive. You are usually a good friend to those in need. You have an emotional power that leads people to tell you their problems often. You have a stern but intelligent character. You seek to rise above yourself and your limitations.

You have great power, perseverance and strength in many areas of your life. You are a force to be reckoned with on any playing field. Your only weakness is a fear of abandonment, you can be deeply loving to your partner and expect the same in return at all costs.

You are extremely complex and crafty; you enjoy shrewd insightful behaviors such as debating or sparring. You have a charming endurance to face any obstacles that have entered your path. You are philosophical and self aware, which typically leads you to the bedroom on many occasions. You can sometimes be a little too selfish or sarcastic for some people to take or understand. Some may see you as the know it all. You are strong willed and courageous when it comes to your goals.

You do not know how to lose and this can make you savagely moody. As a lover you are jealous, possessive and controlling to the point of emotional imprisonment of your partner. If you are suspicious of another's indiscretions you are one sign that is very prone to violence when jealous or angry. You are most compatible with, Cancer, Pisces, and other Scorpios; although two Scorpios may be too demanding on each other.

Pisces
February 20th-March 20th
Power Color: Heliotrope, Planet: Neptune

You are sensitive, vulnerable and imaginative. You are insecure and intense on many levels; you love high drama and crave being the damsel in distress more than you would like anyone to know.

You are very creative and have a good sense of humor. You are naturally gifted in the areas of music and the arts. You have a passive aggressive personality that keeps you from moving on from true emotional security. Your life is a constant search for more meaningful foundations. You are more spiritual than some other signs, and seek a higher sense of the universe and self. You tend to pick the wrong person for you over and over again while you are waiting for your prince to come and rescue you from all the playboys.

You tend to always want what you can't have. You tend to be a passive person that enjoys the escapes of drugs, alcohol, and love affairs to keep your ideas of fantasy more realistic to you. You tend to be dishonest and unfaithful with your partners but expect them to be honest and faithful to you. Pisces have a tendency to take friends to bed and act like nothing happened. 'What? Of course we are still only friends why?' If you are looking to begin a solid relationship you need to take a hard look at your monogamous capabilities or find someone who doesn't mind sharing. Pisces are most compatible with Cancer's Scorpio, and other Pisces; although another Pisces will double your chances of infidelity.

THE AIR SIGNS

Gemini:
May 22nd-June 21st
Power Color: Yellow, Planet: Mercury

You are quick, clever, witty and charming. You are indecisive and often late because you can't make up your mind about where you want to go. Your mind is restless and impatient. After you finally make up your mind, you change it.

You are difficult, demanding and changeable and critical in the area of love. You are well liked by others but sometimes superficially. You would rather be at a party or with friends at work than always alone. You love to be constantly entertained by the next thought, person, and place to go. You are more compulsive than you are spontaneous and those close to you tend to be frustrated by your capricious nature. It is difficult for you to follow through on promises or finish projects without becoming detached or bored. You are a mischievous flirt, but you test without really wanting the quiz at the end.

You are impatient and fickle in many areas of your life. Your sense of humor tends to make you the center of attention and children adore your child like nature. It is difficult for you to remain faithful because you just can't make up your mind. You feel life is a ride and not a destination, so it is difficult for you to really settle down until later in life.

You tend to lack compassion and can be cruel when in an argument. You need to choose carefully whom you would like to settle down with or you will become bored quite easily. Gemini's are most compatible with Aquarius, Libra's and other Gemini's; although another Gemini will double your chance of infidelity.

Aquarius:
January 21st-February 19th
Power Colors: All, Planet: Uranus

You are very curious and friendly like a modern day Alice in wonderland. You are very analytical and idealistic. You are a very good listener, and gossip is a guilty pleasure for you. You thrive on excitement and love the unusual. You do not understand lazy or narrow minded people and try to avoid them when possible. You tend to be very trusting and honest in your relationships.

You like romance, but with open communication and inspiration from your partner. Your ideas can be a bit scattered and overly emotional but you are probably a caring humanitarian and friend. You tend to live your life like an absent minded professor, so caught up in what's going on with those around you that you cannot see what is right in front of your nose. You tend to let your own life pass you by while you are waiting for something magical to happen in your own.

You are sincere but fickle, and are not the greatest fan of a typical work environment. You do not like to feel stifled or bossed around. Your social consciousness makes you a great activist or inventor. Because you are very independent you tend to marry later in life, when you feel your curiosities with others have finally been satisfied.

Because you love your freedom, you cannot tolerate a partner that is obsessively jealous or controlling. No one will posses you, they will only be allowed to be along for the ride... Aquarius is most compatible with Gemini, Libra and another Aquarius, although Libras may be too clingy for your taste.

Libra:
September 24ᵗʰ-October 23ʳᵈ
Power Color: Indigo, Planet: Venus

You are charming, sociable and humorous. You are a romantic at heart and have a loving, warm personality. You love parties and creativity as much as you do emotional security.

You hate being taken for granted, and crave love and attention. You are a sensualist and pleasure seeker who doesn't usually enjoy living alone. You are idealistic and seek a loving, committed relationship. You have a difficult time communicating what you really want and need, because you are so worried about taking control of your own life.

You do not recognize readily that you have a right to think, act and be a certain way without stepping on someone else's ego.

You tend to get bossed around a bit more than other signs because of your inability to stand up for yourself on a regular basis. You crave creature comforts and want to be surrounded by a sense of accomplishment in your home life and career. Even though you are romantic, you tend to be a fickle lover if you are not in a deep committed relationship. You tend to be drawn to superficial things in your mate, and then bore of them quite easily.

You tend to be more in love with the very idea of love than with the actual person. You have the tendency to be self serving in your relationships. Libras are most compatible with other Libras, Aquarius and Gemini's, although a Gemini's changeable flaky nature may make you feel too insecure.

"The signs you ignore, are the gifts you have thrown away"......

Angela DeVere

The Music Mini Test

If you have a varied music library collection from classical, alternative, rock, hip hop and R&B, you may want to reconsider the guy that only listens to country and or only watches CMT. This could be a clear indication that he is narrow minded about many aspects of his life. If you ride in the car together pay attention to the music and radio stations he naturally chooses. There of course is nothing wrong with country music or CMT, I'm just trying to say that if he only listens to any one kind of music genre, he may not have as open a mind as you might prefer.

If you get a chance to see his cd collection or iPod look to see if he only has one or few music types. Unless that is if you only have 1 or few genres that are the same, in that case...well go out for karaoke one night and surprise him with a song from your favorite CD..

If he listens to certain songs/music that are overly offensive or poppy he may be trying to show he can fit in to the "it" crowd. If he chooses music that is politically in correct or preachy he my swing a little father right or left than you might like. Just pay attention, I'm sure you will find it interesting to see what his music says about his personality and taste.

The Big 3

It is important to basic harmonious compatibility that you share at least three ideals and or activities in common. Relationships can sometimes work if you are complete opposites, but fundamental value differences such as religion and finances will cause tension, arguments and deep seated grudges if you are not completely understanding and accepting of your partner's philosophies.

Once again, finding someone that shares your basic beliefs and has the same interests, is much easier on your heart and your chances of success, than trying to change them into someone you want them to be.

For example: If one of you is very religious and or wants a big family, chances are dating someone who may be non-religious and is worried about overpopulating the planet is just a philosophical and family value argument waiting to happen.

You are both entitled to your own beliefs and they should be respected, but all things considered, an atheist that snowboards in France and practices Yoga every morning dating a born again Christian that hates to fly and exercise are about as likely to get along as a Rat and a Boa Constrictor. ...

If you are dating someone that you do not share *at least* three ideals and or activities with, you may want to ask yourself what it is that you are trying to achieve. Are you just settling, hoping they will someday change, or trying to piss off your ex or parent with someone you know they would hate? Be careful. Unless you are a big fan of drama, divorce and depression, you are better off being without a partner for awhile if your frame of mind includes any of the above.

It's all in your head…

According to the rules of selective perception chances are two to one at any given point and time that one's perception is inwardly focused.

Because of our personal biases which stem from a combination of genetic traits and past experiences, how we view people, thoughts, conversations, relationships etc. can be oftentimes viewed from a tainted perspective. Human traits such as height, weight, eye color and predisposition to certain illnesses are all predetermined by our genetic code

Learning to recognize, utilize and sometimes counteract our indulgent perceptions can help us to learn effective and improved communication; as well as teach us how to identify the healthiest types of relationships for our own personality types and genetic make ups.

.

There are many aspects as to what makes someone attractive to us, physical attraction is just one piece. To be able to look beyond our learned behavior biases and within ourselves to see and recognize what true compatibility is comprised of is the key to relationship happiness. Don't just expect e-harmony to figure it out for you and send you the monthly bill, take some ownership of your individual compatibility issues and learn from them. If you don't know who *you* really are or what influences *your* choices in life, you cannot identify with whom you should really share it with. In order for a relationship to be interdependent, happy and lasting, it takes two people who each know themselves well enough to know the difference.

Stop and ask yourself what three things physically in a mate makes them seem attractive to you, and then take some time to figure out why, you should really write them down.

Why do you like tall dark and handsome, or blondes? What are you really trying to achieve when you pursue what physically attracts you? Are you trying to prove something to yourself, to your parents, the universe? Take some time to be introspective and honest. Be sure the desire stands from something real and not from an unhealthy learned behavior.

Now that we have examined the many facets of basic compatibility, let's reflect on what got us into this situation to begin with. Have you been too romantically obsessed with wanting a fairy tale to see the true nature of not only the man in front of you but of your own reflection?

Have you forgotten that men really do think differently than us, and that sometimes we need to wipe our glittery tears and listen with our hearts *and* our minds?

Have you babied your man, and then scolded him the next day for being immature and ungrateful? Were you ever attracted to a selfish playboy and ended up in an unhappy relationship because you thought that you could change him?

I hope that this chapter has given you the tools and self realization check you needed to see that we need to stop blaming it all on the men. Our pattern of enabling has caused most of them to be the type of guy that we now despise. In fact, often couples I have spoken with are sadly in a relationship where they feel they have "settled" just to be in one.

Many "settled" partners feel obligated because of time spent together which sometimes causes too much guilt to just let it go; but what one or both parties don't realize is that the one who "settled" will either eventually be unfaithful to fill a void or often leave the relationship completely when they find what it is they are really looking for in a mate. Don't be the "safe" person in the relationship that gets used over and over again while they are shopping for someone else behind your back. FYI, you shouldn't do that to anyone else either, what goes around comes around. Karma really can be a bitch.

We as women need a reality check on every level to wake up out of our sleeping beauty mentality and demand to be treated as well as we deserve. It is not until you love yourself enough to stand up to the sociopaths, and playboys of the world, that you will ever find a man who will respect you enough to love you for the woman you are.

Do you want to be a servant or a queen? That decision is completely up to you.

CHAPTER 1 BASIC COMPATIBILITY TEST

1. What top 3 things make him attractive to you?
    (2 pts for honesty)_____   _____   _____

2. Do you have at least 3 basic ideals or activities in common? i.e.:
    Religious/Political Views, Hobbies, Educational Background?

    Yes =5 pts_____   Less than 2 =0_____

3. Is there anything about him you feel you want to change now
    or later?
    Yes = 1 pt. _____ No = 4 pts for compatibility_____

4. Does he have more than 5 characteristics of a sociopath?
    (Subtract 5 for Yes) -_____

5. Do you feel like you need to be in a relationship at all costs even
    if you are not happy?
    (Subtract 2 for Yes) -_____

6. Does he have the same narrow or open mindedness as you in
    music and philosophy?
    Yes = 2 pts_____

7. Does your gut tell you that he is trustworthy? BE HONEST?
    Yes 3 pts_____

8. Is his Zodiac sign in your compatibility grouping?
    Yes 2 pts _____

9. Does he stare deeply at you, and lean in during conversations?
    Yes = 3 pts_____

10. Does he make you smile, and still show through his *actions* that
he cares?
    Yes = 3 pts_____

Total_____

20-25 is a very compatible score and you two are off to a great start

15-19 is workable compatibility, but you may want to re-evaluate what you are looking for in him

10-14 is not the best match, he may have some issues that you should avoid

0-9 pts Run away, but don't tell him where you're going....

Chapter 2
Chivalry and Truth, When Boys act like Boys

Giovanna's Famous Boy Math

My good friend Giovanna, has the perfect truth meter test for any men you are dating.

Take what a man says to you, divide it in half, take that half and divide it in half again and 5% of that will equal the truth. ☺

When we take a closer look at romantic heroic tales of old, it is interesting to note that the chivalrous knight in shining armor whose very duty entailed an oath to hold up the chastity and honor of his lady fair, is usually the one that ended up taking her to bed to "save" her from the horny king and end her *miserable* virginity himself.

This combination of lustful male altruism and female enamored naivety is the bread of life to those that seek a happy relationship of three months to a few years. True compatibility is what is still there when the fairy dust, endorphins and hormones fall away, and you still kind of like each other anyway.

Some people get lucky every once in awhile, but I recommend getting to know him better than just the player fronting game he used to get you into bed, and thoroughly check underneath the silver suit before you get too swept away.

A women's intuition is a great gift, how many times has your intuition told you that a guy was lying, even when he swears he's not; only to find out later that you were right all along? If they can create doubt in your mind, "usually by telling you you're suspicions are crazy", then he will work the magic tap dance of denial on you every time.

We need to trust our instincts and use our minds a little more often in our decision making instead of just listening to what our emotionally deprived hearts want; or what their manipulative lust driven lips may say to play on our heart strings.

The following are some insights and behavior clues to watch out for, especially if your spidey senses are telling you that he's full of crap.

Clues:

First of all, if you are ever discussing a friend of yours who just got cheated on, and your man's first response is, "So how did he get caught?" You may want to guard your heart ladies; this guy's just taking notes. If he is already flaky and shady after a few outings it means he probably likes to play games. This is the serial dater with lots of ladies in his pocket. Quite frankly the first hot woman that catches his eye that day is the one he probably takes home later. That is what he means by "we'll see;" to your movie invitation. In other words if he hasn't had any better or "new" offers by the end of the day he will definitely give you a call.

Any man who really is really interested in getting to know you would not be flaky about it. If he says repeatedly after a few dates when you ask about future plans to get together again something like, "I'll let you know", let him know asap that you will be busy for the rest of the week. Do not call him for a few weeks, better yet, let him call you. If his behavior continues to be flaky after that, move on to someone who isn't trying to behave like he is still in high school. If he just "Isn't that into you." Please don't waste your time trying to convince him of anything otherwise. You are probably doing yourself a favor to walk away.

This type of personality obviously needs some time to grow up before he can truly spend time in anyone else's life. Because other women have tolerated his manipulative and boyish behavior before, he will assume that you will do the same. If nothing else comes of it, by giving him the boot you have taught him that not all women are mere subservient playthings.

He will eventually (maybe at 70) reach a point in his life when he tires of games, and he will finally know the right woman to start looking for; the one who is smart enough to call him out on his own game. There is no need to pursue anything that you don't really want and besides, please remember that everything you chase in life runs away. Stand your ground and let someone worthwhile pursue you.

Pants on Fire? The worst thing we can do when it becomes obvious that they are playing games or lying to us is to just let it go. What exactly are you waiting for? To be lied to seven or eight times and then say something? By then it is too late. Call him out on his BS as soon as you feel it is happening. Look him in the eye, tell him you know he is lying and that he can talk to you again when he is ready to be open and honest. If he comes back ready to talk and be sincere, great; if he doesn't well you just saved yourself from being lied to and hurt in the future and taught him to respect you. Trust your instincts. An easy way to identify a liar is by their body language. When someone is lying they send non-verbal cues. If you are skilled enough to look for them you will be able to protect yourself better against being played.

Posture

A very stiff and rigid posture can be a sign that someone's lying (particularly if this way of standing isn't normal for them). They may shift from foot to foot – their posture actually looks nervous or uncomfortable.

Hands

Someone telling a lie tends to make fewer gestures, (ironically, because they're worried their gestures will give them away). This is why some people put their hands in their pockets (or clench them tightly together) when they're telling a lie – it's a way of ensuring their hands stay under control.

Feet and Arms

Look out for a sudden crossing of the arms or legs, particularly if the person does it just as they tell what you think is a lie.

Touching the Face

The ultimate sign of a lie is covering the mouth while speaking. Look for touches of the mouth, or more commonly the nose, ear or chin (it's interesting to note how many people get an 'itchy nose' or chin while lying.)

Direction

Many people actually turn away from the listener when lying. If they are sitting, instead of facing you directly they will turn slightly to the side and speak as if there is someone standing behind you

(Body Language, Jane Lyle).

According to Stephany Alexander the founder of womensavers.com, there are ten signs to look for when your man is cheating.

1. He spends less time with you. A cheating man must use the excuse of working long hours, extra meetings and dinners or other unexplained functions so he will have time with his "other" woman.

2. He isn't as affectionate any more. Your sex life is almost non-existent because of his other commitments. He doesn't want to cuddle, watch a movie, hold hands or do many of the touchy things he used to.

3. He changes his physical appearance. A cheating man usually starts buying new clothes, gets a new hair style or begins working out because he wants to be attractive to the other woman in his life besides you.

4. Car changes. The passenger seat in the car has been moved or there is an unknown hair on the car seat. Perhaps the radio station is on an irregular station because that's what she likes.

5. The cheating man becomes more short-tempered because of the guilty feelings as a result of the infidelity. Things that usually did not bother them suddenly start bothering them.

6. A cheating man may smell of perfume, smoke or alcohol, especially if he hasn't had time to change them from meeting with her.

7. Behavioral changes. A cheating man frequently becomes defensive when questioned about his whereabouts. He may turn it around to accuse you of being insecure, possessive or snoopy.

8. Cell phone changes. A cheating man cannot leave his telephone turned on when with you because his other woman may phone him. He may leave the room to have a telephone conversation or say strange things after he picks up a message from his lover. Watch for calls in the middle of the night. If you have access to his telephone bill, check it closely. Look for repeated unknown numbers, times and durations.

9. Computer usage changes. A cheating man may utilize a computer to seek out partners or communicate with. If your man is on his computer for long periods of time at night and he closes the door so you won't see him, he may be communicating or chatting with his other love interest.

10. Changes in spending habits. You can tell if your man is cheating if he is suddenly always broke. He's broke because he is spending all of his money on the other woman. Watch as to whether he is paying with cash and making more frequent ATM withdrawals to cover his paper trail. Check any receipts, bill's or stubs that you may have access to. Once you know if your man is cheating or not, make sure you have a plan of action that you will take after you accuse him. You need to decide whether it's time for you to move on or whether this relationship may be worth a second chance.

Don't push it, or you will push him away……..
According to Christian Carter, the male author of Catch Him and Keep Him, our female suspicions that a man says one thing but really means something quite different are sadly correct. Christian studied many men's behavior and male psychology while researching his book. His interpretation of the following famous male cop out is as follows:

When a man says, **"I don't want a serious relationship right now."**

What he really means is : "I only want a relationship with a woman who already has her act together, is attractive, healthy, independent, easy-going, confident, and who is emotionally in control of herself and her own life. When we're together I want her to share her feelings and challenge and inspire me to keep her love and interest, and to be a great man...but I also want her to know how to do this without trying to change me or turning our relationship into more work and less fun than I can have on my own."

Because many men end up feeling trapped into a relationship, they stray fairly quickly. Don't be such a girl and push or beg for a serious relationship two or three weeks into dating someone. If a few months go by and you are still hitting it off that would be a much better time to see if the two of you are ready to see each other exclusively. Be sure both of you are ready for a serious relationship before you jump into "the talk".

Got that ladies? write it down…

Pumpkin Eaters

Infidelity, as we all now know, is a very prevalent problem in our country, (65% of married men, and now 40% of married women say they have cheated on their spouses at least once). Besides the alarming health risks of a cheating partner who may be spreading std's or even aids, a cheating partner can have many negative effects on your psyche as well. It is wise for us to look into why so many of us stray from our partners, and not to just focus on how to catch them cheating. Infidelity can occur for many reasons, boredom, sexual addictions; emotional needs are not being met, unfulfilled psyche issues, revenge, the challenge, or just the game.

When people begin a serious relationship too quickly, without considering all aspects of compatibility besides a basic sexual attraction; the passion in the bedroom fades quickly and you are left with a void. Because you don't necessarily hate the other person, and you don't want to hurt anyone's feelings you may keep them around as a sort of safety net or back up plan. But if you are feeling any of the above, your eyes may soon begin to stray, and when that happens, your body may soon begin to follow.

According to research on Savvymale.com, "Studies on brain chemistry and hormonal responses support the notion that the early courtship period is bolstered with ignition and heated biochemical reactions". These reactions, much like the brains response to chocolate, create a biochemical glue that's supports a couples' early relationship. It can last up to 3 years and then slowly dies. This may explain why most married couples complain of the 5 or 7 year itch. If they have nothing of substance to fall back on they may opt to leave when the good vibes wear off. Some other interesting statistics on cheating are that 15-20% are repeat offenders, 15-20 % say they go to church or are religious, 50-75% of affairs happen with someone from the workplace, 50-70% of marriages end up in divorce, only 10-15 % of marriages succeed after infidelity counseling, and 99.9% of cheaters say they will deny, deny, deny it…unless, you can prove it!

The most psychologically damaging part of an affair is experienced by the "victim" of the cheating partner. After cheating occurs, and comes out in the open it becomes difficult, if not impossible to rebuild the same level of trust that once existed between you. It is also very difficult for the victim to learn to trust their own judge of character again with anyone else. The victim begins to wonder what they may have done wrong, they lose self esteem, and may become isolated or depressed for extended periods of time before they are able to come to terms with their partner's betrayal.

If you have been cheated on, take some time to heal yourself before you try and move on too quickly with your next partner. Be sure any relationship you begin is for the right reasons, and not to fill a void. You may consider relationship counseling if you feel your partner's apology is sincere and you are both ready to work on your problems. Remember like anything in life that is worth having, if you truly care about someone and want them to be happy; it takes work, sacrifice, humor, forgiveness and love. You cannot put a relationship on auto pilot and walk away after promises or even vows. It is a choice for both of you to make to decide to stay together, because one happy person in a relationship is not a relationship at all.

Chivalry Before and *after* Sex

Well, well, well, so your man brought you flowers and hugs on the first two dates, chocolate and a kiss on the third, and wine and dancing on the fourth. But after you finally slept with him last Friday, the next day he didn't even remember to open the damn car door. Sound vaguely familiar?

Well remember what my great grandmother used to say about men getting what they want and then not wanting it anymore? The same rule applies here...sort of.

Oh, he still wants the sex, but he views you now much differently now. To men, the chase is always the exciting part. Is it going to take three dates to get you in the sack or ten? After men reach a goal of any kind they celebrate heartily and then they relax. Think of a touchdown for instance, he raced down the football field while avoiding the defensive line, caught the ball, ran to the end zone, and now all he wants is a victory dance, a beer and a long nap.

Don't be fooled into believing they will "like" you more if you sleep with them on the first or second date. They may be sexually frustrated a little longer, but subconsciously if you are too easy they will probably lose respect for you and keeping looking for Mrs. Right elsewhere. As soon as a man believes he has "caught" you, whether it be sexually or even emotionally; his romantic behavior will usually go from Don Juan to "Hey sweetie, you wanna play Nintendo tonight or just get bizzeh?" This is usually the point in the relationship when women wonder why they didn't become a nun.

If the guy you are with does not seem to ever want to take an active role in sharing common activities, mutually pleasing sex acts, or anything that closely resembles good manners, remind him subtly that he hasn't really caught a damn thing and go out for drinks with the girls.If he still hasn't gotten the hint by the time you return, leave a copy of this book on his side of the bed and tell him your best friend just wrote a book about how to break up with selfish immature guys…You're welcome.

When researching the information on body language and "playerisms", I decided to ask some of my friends and acquaintances about their experiences with dishonest men, and how they were able to catch them in a lie. They each of course had hilarious and bittersweet tales of cheating, lies, investigative spy work and cataclysmic endings.

It is great for us to learn from not only our own mistakes, but from others who have paid the price before us. The following stories are true, only the names have been changed to protect the identity of the big fat liars.

The Beep

I'll always remember hitting REWIND on an old answering machine at my boyfriend's apartment.

With each recorded voice, I could hear my life cracking apart like hot water thrown on an icy windshield!

Beep.
"Hi, it's Karen. Had fun the other night. Call me!"

Karen? Why does that name sound so familiar? Karen. (Scan brain). Karen.

Maybe the better question is, why was I alone inside my boyfriend's apartment rewinding my old answering machine I had given him a few months ago?

Sam, the man who surprisingly knew my Karen, my hairdresser, had injured his back while on vacation with his family. He had asked me to feed his cats, pickup his mail and gather some personal things for him.

Beep.
"Hi, Sam, it's Stephanie. I'm so sorry to hear that Melanie's Mom died. That was SO sweet of you to go. Call me, 'kay?"

Stephanie? STEPHANIE? The receptionist at my office?
Melanie? Me.

Sam? Oh, Steph, Sam, or SAMUEL, as I called him for seven years, went to my mother's funeral two weeks ago to serve as a pallbearer. Sorry he had his hands full Step-a-me!

Before the next soul-crushing **Beep,** I found myself screaming. Alone. In HIS apartment. Screaming the names, Karen? STEPHANIE? STEPHANIE???? Oh my God, Karen? The tart whom I trusted with work secrets, man trouble and most importantly, highlights?! Why would the 20-something, tall, lean, gorgeous, smoker, ice-skater Karen call my boyfriend?

Beep
"Samuel, its Tina. What's up? Call me."
Tina....Tina...Tina?! Tina?
Tina my videotape editor.
WHAT?
They KNOW each other?
Like, really, KNOW each other?
We had just seen Tina at the Silver Creek Music Festival in the mountains outside Denver.
Tina has a BABY.
She's married? Right? No wait, she's getting a divorce, I think.

That's a little tease of my story. It's a true story. At age 44, I'm finally able to laugh about it.
I'm almost able to giggle about breaking a window, being handcuffed to a hospital bed and going to jail over this.
Okay, so I had a little freak out.

Confronted Sam. Threw my car keys at him. He slammed the door on me. I hit his apartment sliding glass window door with my fist. It shattered. Next thing I know, neighbors call police. In Colorado, where Sam slept with all of my "friends", one of the partners in a domestic disturbance MUST be carted off by police and questioned. It's the law.
Since I was the key throwing, fist jabbing, furious and bloodied aggressor, I was chosen by authorities to step into an ambulance for treatment. And so on........

Anyway, it's a true story.
I was in media at the time.
That old boyfriend?
He is now Vice President of Media Affairs for
PLAYBOY.

Melanie, Colorado

The Trip

I grew up in Northern California, a typical happy childhood where I dreamed of meeting my prince charming one day. I thought I had found true love at the end of my senior year. I met my ex boyfriend Jacob at a Community center dance in 1999. We hit it off right away. I thought I had found my perfect college sweetheart. We spent almost every day together and he seemed to genuinely care for me. He talked about our mutual future together after college pretty often so I naturally assumed we would eventually marry.

After about eight months of serious dating Jacob said he needed to go to Fresno to visit his sick grandfather for about 6 weeks. I was quite sad because I knew I would miss him terribly but I understood the situation and wished him well. I even made him a card and said I would pray for his grandfather's health. We spoke each week at least a few times on the phone until the last few weeks when he seemed to call a lot less. I didn't think much of it at the time, I just thought his excuses of being really busy with family and old friends to not be any big deal. When he came back to town, I was so happy but he seemed somehow different and distant.
He was happy to see me and all, but I could sense he was holding back. He seemed over the next few weeks to get angry and upset a lot more often about silly things, and said he just needed some space. I was angry and hurt but I agreed. We didn't speak for about a week until he called one night to say he missed me and that he was sorry for being a jerk. He said he felt like I was "pushing"

him into something he just wasn't ready for yet.. Funny thing is before he left he was the one who was pursuing me. I told him I would try and give him a few weeks to figure out what he really wanted and he agreed.

Of course there was no answer/ phone call back EVER. So after being preempted (by such a dear friend) I decided or better yet we decided it would be a good idea to drive by his house just to see what was going on. Although I already know what you're thinking PHYSO I feel we are all aloud to make one bad judgment call.

So against my better judgment we decided to drive by. As we entered his street we noticed some flickering lights coming from the half opened curtains. I instructed or more so demanded Jamie (my dear friend) to pull over. We parked down the street (obviously) and walked closer to the house to get a better look. As I peered through the window (wow I feel so creepy now) sure enough there it was: A little music playing ever so softly, with candles and rose petals spread throughout the entire house. I was in shock for the first few minutes' then anger swept over me. I looked at Jamie and she knew exactly what I was going to do. I started pounding on the door but there was no answer. Apparently he was picking up his "company" for the night. So like what many other 18-year-olds, I decided to go home and get up REAL early the next morning and go back over. I figured anything he was doing that night would still be going on the next morning.

As my alarm boomed at 6 am I was up like a shot and on my way to find out what was going on. When I got to the house the music was off, candles blown out, but all the flowers lay exactly how I had seen them. I began pounding on the door (I know not my finest moment) but I had to know. After about 10 minutes of crazy knocking a dreary ever so tired ex -boyfriend opened the door. I will never forget the look on his face one of shear shock and a little enjoyment. I tore past him and much to my surprise found an empty bedroom with blankets all over the floor. After calling me crazy for the next few moments he reassured me all the flowers were for his MOM. Oh please! I left that day with little dignity but my head held high. Although I didn't know then whom the flower display was for or the bright lit candles I sure got one hell of a story out of it!. It turns out he had met up with his ex girlfriend in Fresno and he had invited her home to try and rekindle their old relationship. Two years later they married and had three children, they were married for six years and then she left him for his best friend who happens to be my favorite cousin John. It seemed his pattern of "winning" a great girl and then still thinking the grass was greener somewhere else was something she had found out the hard way too.

Submitted by Melissa Byron

Being happy in a relationship doesn't mean everything is perfect
It means you have decided to see beyond the imperfections or wise
enough to avoid them all together.

As we have just read sometimes the sociopath personalities can fool us for awhile, but most men are horrible liars. They have the funniest way of giving answers to simple questions like: "Why didn't you answer your phone all night?"

Their answer: "Well I left my charger in my cubicle, and then I dropped my phone in the shower when I got home and it got wet, so by the time I used my roommates blow dryer to get it working again, I figured you'd be sleeping, so I didn't call you back." As a woman, you sit back in amazement and wonder how long did it take him to come up with that?. The funny thing is that this same man when asked where he wants to go on your next date will say, "I don't know, I'm not that good at planning stuff."

Men lie because nine times out of ten they are doing something that they know you would disapprove of. Once the lies began, there is usually no end in sight. Even when they are given an opportunity as a friend and lover to come clean, most will still deny any wrongdoing because of macho swag and pride. The thing men don't seem to realize is that unless they are dating a total airhead, (which is usually what they settle for) their lies will always be exposed, eventually.

Men lie for different reasons depending on the situation. Say for instance, he went out the night before, he met up with friends and went to a bar, and he ends up with a telephone number that he has no recollection of getting. While you are doing laundry you find it in his pants pocket. Instead of telling the truth about how he obtained it, he will give you the tall tale version of events! It is easier to tell a lie in their eyes than to face the consequences of the truth. On the downside, some men want their cake and eat it too when protecting their infidelities. It may be necessary to turn into your personal version of CSI and conduct your own investigation. The look on a man's face when you unveil their untruths is: *priceless.*

If men would just realize that we are much more likely to stay in a relationship with someone who is honest with us, instead of making up little lies about everything they think will cause an argument; it would be much easier for us to communicate effectively. It would also be less painful for everyone in the end. Men often say they hate drama but because of their boyish dishonest behavior, they often bring it on themselves. My personal favorite when catching a lying cheater is to see him hit the hard realization that his sweet friend and lover outsmarted him and he will never taste her beautiful ingenious lips again...

"I guess some men just never learn that yes you can pay for school papa, but you can *never* buy class."- Muah

Stop looking for wannabe prince ladies, what you really want…is a king.

If chivalry is truly dead, and our princes and knights are but evaporating figments of our imagination; we must still remember that if we choose to be queens in this life we will want nothing less than a true king as a life partner. I asked my eleven year old daughter Hannah what a true King should be like and this was her answer.

"A King should be fair, and love his people and treat his queen very good with respect and love; he should not be prideful or snobby or lie to his people or his queen. He should always keep his promises." And what should you do if he doesn't keep his promises, and treat you with love and respect Hannah?

"Tell him he is fired and you're getting a new king named Cody."

Hannah Kershner age 11

Sounds like great advice to me, so let's not make this any more difficult than it is.

And if any of you know a nice guy named Cody, hook me up.

Hannah's Drawing

CHAPTER 2 TEST BASIC COMPATIBILITY TEST

1. On your first few dates did he act with chivalry and display manners?
Yes =10 pts _____

2. Do your spidey senses tingle when he is telling you where he was last night?
Yes Subtract 5 _____

3. Is his behavior often shady, flaky or unreliable?
Yes Subtract 5 pts. _____
.
4 Has he exhibited any lying body language when being asked a direct question?
No = 10 pts -_____

5. After having sex, are his chivalry and manners still intact?
Yes = 5 pts _____

6. Does he seem to be overly protective of his phone, or turn it off late at night?
Yes Subtract 5 pts. -_____

7. Does he show any behavioral signs of a serial cheater/player?
No =10 pts _____

8. Have you learned to better identify player behavior and call him out on it the very first time?
Yes= 10 pts. _____

9. Have you memorized Giovanna's Boy Math Formula?
Yes =5 pts. _____

Total _____

40-50 Kudos, your man is reliable and honest until proven guilty

20-39 Nice Sleuthing Carmen San Diego, keep a close eye on him or move on

0-19 . Call this *&^%$# out on his BS, and delete his number. He is so not worthy

Chapter 3

The 1 hr Sexual "Torture" Test

Warning Sexually Explicit Material

Aha, you skipped ahead to this page for a preview… ☺

Believe me when the time comes for you to use this test you will not be disappointed by the telling clues it will give you about the inner workings of your man.

As you have reached a point in any dating relationship where you are ready to become a little more sexually active with your partner, this test will allow you to role play, to see if he can share power and follow simple directions and more importantly if he can please *you* in the bedroom.

As you are preparing for this test, remember that he will not be able to please you and share his life fully in a relationship if he cannot let you be in control of his body and mind for one simple hour.

The body is easy, what man doesn't want some sexy vamp bondage time?
The real test comes with his mind….

Note: Use it only on those men who you are truly interested in. It is a great tool to check your life partner compatibility with someone and a good indication of how he can perform under pressure. Psychologically speaking, this test is designed to make sure your man is not a control freak; to see if he recognizes that your power as a woman and your pleasure is just as important as his; to see if he can keep an open mind, is open to new experiences, has a good sense of humor, and of course study his sexual performance. ..You're Welcome.

Step 1
15 minutes

Set the scene......this is a surprise test, so don't spoil it by giving him clues about the quiz he is going to be in for.

Order pizza, make dinner, or go to dinner depending on what you prefer; And depending on whose dish night it is.

Let him know that the mood is right by your flirtatious innuendo, deep stares, and slowed speech. If you drink alcohol, a few glasses of wine or cocktails might not be a bad idea, at least it helps with the slowed speech.....

Wear something particularly revealing as this is an automatic clue to men who are sexually stimulated visually that you are ready for a romp in the hay.
Have these items in a night table or under a pillow (at your place or hotel) ready for easy access: Stiletto Heels, 1 Necktie, Massage oil, Honey, and Condoms. Wear one extra necktie underneath your clothes as part of the surprise.

After dinner...and a few sexual clues later, head towards your testing area.
Tell him to take a quick shower and (wash thoroughly) for reasons that will become obvious as you continue reading. You may sit in the bathroom and continue your flirting and innuendo while you wait. After he's finished, help him dry off, and kiss him deeply, telling him you want him.

As you enter the bedroom, make sure your kisses are passionate and full of desire, tell him to lie down on the bed and to watch you quietly as you undress slowly, if he speaks while you are stripping, gently lean over and kiss his mouth and whisper shhhh....

He will be surprised to see that you are undressing down to just a necktie and excited by the prospect that you must have had this erotic surprise planned.

Slip on your heels, and tell him to close his eyes. Prepare your honey, extra necktie, condoms and honey. Place them on the bed next to him where he can see it and tell him to open his eyes. Explain to him you are going to tie him up for a test.

So what is the test?
That you are going to do whatever you want to his body, but he cannot speak a word…not even one..for one hour. Sounds easy enough, but believe me, this is no simple schoolgirl assignment.

Slyly reassure him he can moan if he wants but if he speaks one word, you will stop and the test will be over with no sex at all. After he agrees, tie his wrists/arms to the bed with the other necktie and kiss him deeply for obeying your commands. Gently kiss him all the way down to his feet and sit at the edge of the bed. Pour a few drops of honey on his toes and start licking and sucking the honey off. Try making mmmm noises for extra effect to let him know how good he tastes…
If he can get through the toes without speaking you are off to a really good start.

However, more than likely when he realizes what he just agreed to at this point, he will throw his head back on the pillow in sexual frustration. Tell him shh…again

Step 2
15 minutes—
Take the massage oil and begin deeply massaging his hands. After his hands are moist rub his hands slowly over your breasts so that your nipples are slightly erect and are glistening wet. It is a good idea to have low lighting with a few candles so he can still see what you are up to.
 Take the honey and dip his right index finger in the honey, give him a sly smile while you put his finger deep into your mouth and suck off the honey slowly. Continue on with his other fingers.

After about 7 minutes, tell him to turn over onto his stomach. He will be mildly uncomfortable because he is tied up but a little pain is ok. Just make sure it's not too tight.

If he is too uncomfortable you can take a moment to loosen his tie. It is highly unlikely that he will try and escape this "torture" so you should be ok.

When he is face down, start at his shoulders with a good massage and work your way down to the lower back, buttocks and calves. When you reach his bottom, use your nails and with one hand scratch him softly from the back of his neck to his backside and then 2 hands down to his feet. This will heighten his senses and nerve endings to prepare him for step 3.

This is the 30 minute mark where things start to get interesting………..

Step 3

15 minutes

Note: Most Men cannot make it through this phase without talking; they will try and call your bluff. DO NOT CAVE IN IF HE SPEAKS! If he does, stop what you are doing, gently kiss him and tell him he can try again some other time. He will be in shock that you are so in control, and you will know that he doesn't take you very seriously,.. yet.

He may have one more opportunity to pass the test a week or so later, but if he fails you should let him go and move on to someone else who is more willing to share, and doesn't feel like he must always be in control. You can find out now or later, the choice is up to you.

1 minute

Take the honey and put a few drops on each butt cheek. Start on the left side and suck it off hard enough to where it feels like a love bite. Then the right.

At this point he is going to find it increasingly difficult to keep his promise of not talking…He may actually start to whimper..

Ask him to turn over onto his back, you may need to assist him, but more than likely he will have an idea of what you have in store next and will obey you very quickly on his own.

This section will take about 4 minutes.

Take some massage oil and begin rubbing his neck, chest stomach, legs and feet.
You will purposefully skip over his genitals and come back to them in a few minutes. Brush by his genital area just enough to entice his longing for some attention to that area.
If he has actually made it this far without saying a word, go back up to his mouth and kiss him for a few moments…telling him he is being very good.

Step 4
This next section is 11 minutes
After his whole body is warmed up, take the honey and slowly drizzle some on his almost erect penis. Don't be shy, …pour enough to make things interesting……
If he doesn't say "oh my God baby", or another expletive at this point your partner is above average in taking direction and sharing control.
Start at the base and gently lick the honey to the top, making sure you leave some for the 1 minute of sucking left that will get him very excited.
If he still has obeyed at this point and has remained quiet, the last 10 minutes are his reward. AND YOURS OF COURSE.
After the oral sex he should be very erect, place the condom carefully on your partner and climb onto him. Whatever you do with him next, is up to you.
Just make sure he stays quiet, "with his words anyway".;)

The fact that he is very excited and that you are feeling very sure of yourself at this point should make the last ten minutes or so of this test a lot of fun for both of you. Enjoy.

Reminder: Use it only on those men who you are truly interested in. It is a great tool to check your possible life partner's compatibility and a good indication of how he can perform under pressure. Don't abuse it, monogamous sex with someone you care about is a much more spiritual and intimate experience than casual sex could ever hope to be.

If you are not this adventurous in the bedroom, you can simply ask him not to talk during old fashioned mission style sex for an hour; but he may assume that means you think he needs to concentrate harder on his game. You can bruise a man's sexual ego easily, be careful what you wish for..

CHAPTER 3 BASIC COMPATIBILITY TEST

1. Did he speak during the test? Be Honest…

No = 25 pts_____

2. Did he seem openly annoyed at losing one hour of control?

Yes subtract 10 pts -_____

3. Did he seem to enjoy sharing control with you?

Yes =5 pts _____

4. Did you enjoy yourself?

Yes = 5 pts_____

5. Was his performance satisfactory?

Yes = 15 pts. _____

Total _____

30-50 pts. Congratulations, you both are happy mentally stable freaks in the bedroom

15-29 pts. Ummm… You may want to try it again

0-9 pts. Please try again…with someone else

> The greatest mistake you can make in life is to be
> continually fearing you will make one.
> Elbert Hubbard (1856 - 1915)

Chapter 4

Potential Problems Big and Small

The typical reaction we have to any crisis is fear; or what is better known as the fight or flight response. In primitive times this thought process was crucial to our survival, but today survival is much more complex. In today's world fear can paralyze our ability to think clearly, solve everyday problems and make simple decisions. Negativity becomes a self fulfilling prophesy, and panic can cause knee jerk and ill advised reactions.

In all of our lives we experience what I like to call hiccups. You know the little gremlin filled days, weeks or sometimes months when nothing seems to go right or according to plan? There comes a time in every woman's life, when even though she struggles to stay afloat and away from trouble; the drama fairy pays her an unwelcome visit.

These annoying hiccups may be caused by various reasons, but how a guy reacts to a crisis can tell you a lot about their patience, generosity, honesty, and loyalty.

Men say many unspoken things without realizing they give away a lot of their hidden psyche while doing so. Maybe someone in your family takes ill, maybe you have car trouble or even get laid off from work right before your next mortgage payment is due. Whatever the crisis or mini crisis may be, how your significant other responds to these moments can be a telling sign as to how emotionally capable or willing he is to be there for you when you really need him.

I'm not saying he should come in on a white steed and whisk you away to the fix it palace or even offer to pay for all of your life's hiccups. Quite the contrary; but what he should offer you are sincere condolences, a ride home, some chicken soup or Nyquil, to help you re-embellish your resume ☺ , and be a shoulder to cry on.

Men and women have the habit of either being taken advantage of or taking advantage of others during these types of situations. Does your man insist on being treated like a 7 year old when he gets sick? Do you?

Remember, it is one thing to expect your loving boyfriend to give you a hand, but he shouldn't have to fix your life. Hiccups are one thing, an emotional and financial nonstop tsunami are quite another. If you have neediness pattern that rains down on your relationship, asking him to hold your umbrella will not be enough. He will quickly tire of your damsel in distress ways and find someone who already has their act together.

That said, if you truly do have a crisis and need your man to step in, ask him sincerely for his help; explain clearly what has happened. If he moves quickly to assist you with whatever you need and cares enough to not expect some sort of retribution from you sexual or otherwise, you have found yourself a worthy mate. Of course however, if your crisis involves borrowing money to fix a problem of your own doing; plan on paying him back within 3-6 months or don't borrow the money at all. You are a big girl now, don't look for your mate to be your parent or guardian or your 24hr ATM. If you are looking for a book that promotes sugardaddy relationships or teaches women to manipulate men by acting innocent and needy, go back to the bookstore or supermarket and pick up a copy of Tween Weekly.

However, if after you explain the situation he cuts you off, or doesn't answer his phone because he was "busy" for two days or expects favors from you as repayment for simple kindness and compassion; he is just Peter Pan incarnate.

I'm sorry Wendy, but he is selfish, immature and not yet capable of carrying on a serious relationship. If he is more worried about what your "crisis" means as an inconvenience to him, he has not yet learned to step out of himself long enough to sincerely empathize with someone else's needs. It is time to move on, you are learning to be a queen and to demand respect and you should expect the same type of love and compassion you are willing to give your king. If he likes to happily take, take, take from you but he very rarely gives;..It is time to leave him in Neverland and fly back home.

Example 1 Falling Flat

Let's say you've been happily dating your snuggly poo for six months and everything is going great. One evening you are driving home from the farmers market and you blow one of your tires along a dark country road, twenty miles from home.

Part 1   Circle One Answer
Be Honest

Do you,
A: Call a parent and ask for help and money?

B: Phone a friend?

C: Call your boyfriend borderline hysterical and beg for him to come and get you?

D: Call Triple A, then your boyfriend to explain what happened and ask if he could pick you up until your vehicles repaired?

You
D: = 5 points
Nicely handled

B: = 2 points
Not a bad choice either

A: = 1 point
Cut the umbilical chica, you are a grown up

C: = 0 points
Step away from the tiara

Part 2

After receiving your phone call, the correct big girl one or (choice D), does he?

A: Not answer his phone 3 times or a respond to your 911 text?

B: Answer but say that he has to go to work or school tomorrow, so just call your mom?

C: Say ok, but then when he arrives he pouts, whines and makes you feel guilty for interrupting whatever else he was doing?

D: He says sure, arrives with hot coffee, a sense of humor and a hug before he drives you home?

His Efforts
A: = 0 points
What a Jerk, I hope he was taking a two hour shower or he blows cookies.

B: = 0 points
What a Punk, especially if your mom needs to get up for work too.

C: = 1 point
What a Baby, did he come with his own eggshells for you to walk on?

D: = 5 points
What's His Number???

(   )_____?

Just kidding ladies, he's a keeper, just see if he has a friend or a brother who is not afraid of commitment, single moms, strong creative sexy published authors, or drinking red wine; I'm not expecting prince charming to pop up on my face book either, so hook a sister up.

Example 2

No Vacancy at the Inn

It is late spring, love is in the air and you and your significant other are doing fabulous. You think you have found true love, the sexiest man alive and your knight in shining armor all rolled into one. You spend a lot of time together, hanging out at each other's houses and sleeping over on a regular basis.

So when you hear one afternoon that your rental house needs major repairs to the roof and flooring and that it won't be habitable for almost two weeks, you call up your bestest buddy and true love and ask him if you can stay over for a few weeks.

It should be a no brainer right? You get to spend more snuggly TV. time together and have twice the great sex as usual, all while saving money on a hotel.

Q&A Circle one answer that matches his actions and behavior

After the call to your understanding Romeo, does he?

A: Say, heck ya, offer to help you pack a few things and ask what groceries you want from the store?

B: Hesitate and say "ok, I guess, but only if it's for two weeks."

C: Say, "No, I don't think so, I had a bad experience with living together before so I don't want to. I promised myself I would not ever get in that kind of situation again."

His Performance

A: = 5 points
To Gryffindor for going above and beyond without making superficial judgments or assumptions. He realizes you are not trying to induce marriage and doesn't freak out.

B: = 3 points
For honesty and healthy independence.
However, if his plan is to never share a roof with a woman longer than two weeks unless he is engaged or married because he says he is a "traditional" guy, remind him it is also traditional to not have sex before marriage and that it is not 1963. This sounds more like a commitment cop out, or a parent fearing/pleasing ideal than a real set of individual values.

C: = 0 points
Unless you have given him a reason to make him think you are exactly like his ex who took advantage of his kindness he needs to move out of the past and stop making assumptions. Furthermore, if he wants you to know what he is really afraid of, he should tell you. Women's intuition isn't quite advanced enough yet to read minds. If he doesn't trust you even though you have not given him any reason not to; he not only has trust and commitment issues, he could very well have something to hide. Proceed with caution.

You're Performance

Faced with an answer of A, would you?

A: Move in happily for two weeks, but then beg to stay longer and guilt him into a roommate situation?

B: Move in and out within the two weeks as agreed?

If you answered: A:= 0 points
You shiesty little devil woman, no, no, no…never be where you are not really wanted.

B: = 5 points
Way to keep your word and not be a clingy leechy princess

Faced with an answer from him of B, would you?

A: Have a talk with him about "traditional" values and not picking one over the other?

B: Just say, ok and never bring up the subject during your two week stay *or* mention that you think his ancient double standard ideas are ridiculous?

A:= 4 points
For being open and honest about your feelings and trying to uncover his.

B: = 0 points
For wasting your time and hoping he will change

Faced with an answer from him of C would you?

Why would you do anything here unless you plan on dating the guy for ten years and then hoping he will finally break down and propose?

My best advice is to let him find out what life is like without you for awhile without making much of it, he may or may not get a clue.

Example 3
Mama Mia

If you have children like I do, you know firsthand how it can affect your social life. Whether you are still in the stages of changing diapers or already handing over the keys, the time and emotional constraints of parenting can be quite a challenge when looking for love. If your beau has been accepting of the fact that you have a child or children in your life and respects your time for parenting, you should be in good shape.

But what if…

You planned a romantic evening for the two of you for Friday night and that afternoon you get a call that your sitter has to cancel because of a sudden illness. Bummed, but calm you call your boyfriend and let him know the situation.

Does your understanding pookie bear;

A: Say ok, not a problem let's just do it another night?

B: Pout and say "Why can't someone else like 'their dad' watch them? I already made reservations."

C: Say, I'm sorry babe, why don't I just bring over a pizza and we can all just watch a movie tonight?

Then, he shows up in 30 minutes or less and brings flowers with the pizzas.

Hey I can dream it's my book. ☺

A:= 3 points

He is understanding and doesn't seem to have a selfish agenda or to be too insecure.

B: = 0 points
Overly emotional and selfish reaction

C: = 10 points
For being dreamy and liking you enough to get to know your family

Question of the day? If it's only a penny for my thoughts, why should I let you put your two cents in?

Kids and Relationships

It may come as a surprise to some of you that those beautiful little bundles of joy that have been your greatest blessing in life may not always be seen as a positive asset by every potential suitor. I'm sure each of you has her own time table as to when you allow the man in your life to be introduced to your little ones, and that is a very personal decision to make. I can only suggest that you wait long enough to uncover any sort of danger or personality flaws that may be a detriment to your children before bringing him around. It can be heartbreaking and traumatic for a child to become attached to someone you are dating only to be disappointed along with you when things begin to fall apart. Remember, it is not just you he is considering adding to his life if you are a mom, you are truly a package deal.

You must look at the men in your life with as much scrutiny as you would for someone that your child is dating. An easy rule to apply here is that if something about him tells you he wouldn't be good enough to theoretically date your sister, your cousin or your daughter, ask yourself why you are keeping him around. Even though he isn't dating them directly, you should learn how to take your own advice and steer clear of losers. A queen doesn't need a jester in her court to help her rule her kingdom, she needs a King.

Some men, especially those who have not yet had children of their own, tend to sadly see other people's children as baggage. This doesn't always mean that they hate or dislike children but that they are unable to step out of their own selfish plan and accept a relationship where there are someone else's children involved.

You know, "THE PLAN", the one where guys finish college, get a great job, buy a great house and then a 24 year old blond supermodel with no kids and a million dollars in the bank rings their doorbell. Yeah, that plan, the one that men contrive in their heads at a young age based not only on their own egos but their innate need to please society or gain peer admiration. The plan that makes it hard for merely pretty, intelligent, funny, sweet women like you and I to be ever be enough. I mean c'mon, as soon as he commits to you and settles down you know she's gonna show up in a bikini in his driveway on her way to the hooter's girl convention looking for a ride. Duh...

As silly and unrealistic as that sounds, that type of male mentality is a lot more common than you might think. If an ignorant man believes he has a chance with a woman like that, an opportunity at the hot wife who would be the envy of the office; even if she is now broke and is using him to pay her way, he will probably take it. If this type of guy has someone in his life or even his dreams that he believes he can have like that, it will not matter how much you have in common or enjoy each other's company, he will not want to commit.

I don't think I need to tell you that a woman with kids doesn't usually fit into "THE PLAN". Since you know on page 346 paragraph B of his plan he and his supermodel wife are going to have children of their own. If you are dating someone who is living in this type of selfish fairy tale mentality stop and ask yourself if he is really the type of "grown up" you want to have as a male role model in your children's lives.

A man like this will never admit openly to you that he wants a prize for peer admiration instead of a truly compatible life partner. But if he still will not commit to you after quite some time with or without children present and your relationship is great, you can bet she is floating around in his head somewhere.

The following is real, an exact copy of a Dear John letter I wrote to someone who was stuck in his "plan". Depending on how much time has passed when this book is published and read, I hope for his sake he has not yet reached a point in his life when he has realized, I was right. ☺

Dear_____

"I'm just tired, tired of being taken advantage of, playing dating games and never seeming to be enough for you. I'm tired of men who think as soon as they make a real commitment, a magical blond supermodel with no kids and a million dollars in the bank is going to show up at their door, so "yeah" they wanna hold off a bit longer before settling on just plain old me. Suck my balls…

When that faky sweet bimbo wife that you just had to have, the one who makes you feel so admired by her and your idiot peers leaves your manipulated ass after three to seven years because she deep down never really wanted you and takes half of your shit including your planned kids, don't sit in disbelief and cry.

Don't think about how compatible we were as lovers and friends. Don't remember back to me telling so I told you so. Remember back to me telling you I told you so you stupid stubborn ass remote control hogging moron. I really loved you.

No, you are not stupid for wanting the best in life. You're not even that stupid for being conned into a marriage with a co-dependant Barbie doll,.. or by your own ego.

You are stupid because;

You could have had me.

Pretty, brutally honest to a fault me.

Me who actually has a degree and a career

Me who already knows how to be a good wife and a mother

Me who was your best friend and shoulder to cry on.

Me who wanted to be your equal in all things and grow old with you.

Me who loved you _____, simply for being you.

You have shown me through your actions that you are more worried about how everything will affect *you* and what other people will think of *you* than about helping and caring for me. That is *not* a friend.

Hmm…Vero Nihil Verius (There is nothing truer than the truth)

I don't deserve to be someone's second choice, whether she exists or not.

I deserve someone who puts me first.

Life is too short to wait for fairy tales, and by the way fairy tales rarely last.

I want something real,

Best of Luck,"

Angela

When will men see the gift in their hands and stop looking to see who may or may not be on the next page? Sadly, most men really do want what they can't have, and when they get it they don't want it anymore. Who knows ladies? Maybe the gold diggers really are the smart ones? When their husbands cheat on them or they desire a better lover and they cry themselves to sleep, at least they can cheer themselves up the next day at Tiffany's lol.

I jest, never, ever think that money and gifts alone equal love. Actions always speak louder than words. Whether you are the one expecting the gifts to be showered upon you like a succubus, or the one giving them away to "win" a leechy prize.;

Learn from your Mistakes.

4 Hints At Making a Blended Family Work

1. Keep an open mind and remain patient, don't expect a Brady Bunch reaction from everyone involved just because that is what you want. Getting to know each other as a family takes time, don't push it or expect the children to see you as a parental part of their lives right away. Listening and remaining calm are key.

2. Make time for your relationship, the happier you remain individually and as a couple the better you can handle family obstacles together. If the children are not fond of the idea they may try to divide and conquer. If you are sure that he is the type of man you want to include in your family, your children will learn to care or at least tolerate him over time. Think about how you would feel if a stranger moved into your child's room and announced that they were staying...forever. How would you feel? None of us are fond of sharing the people we love, children are no exception.

3. Focus on the positive, be thankful for each other on a daily basis. Don't make assumptions or judgments about an absent biological parent, especially in front of the children. Even if the absent parent is a big selfish loser, he or she is still the child's parent and should be treated with the same respect that you would like to be given to you.

4. Don't spoil or baby the children to "win" them over. Healthy happy children need love, understanding, patience, guidelines, time spent, food, shelter, laughter and *then* X-box games or candy; *not* the other way around.

Personality Profile

A great approach to better identify the needs, values and attitudes of someone you are dating, is to take a closer look at their behavior. There are four main types of personalities. You can sometimes be one personality type in particular or more often a combination of a few.

You should easily be able to pick out after reading through these which personality dominates your thoughts and behavior. Practice using these methods on family and friends before you attempt to expertly identify your dates possible attributes or flaws. It will help you to more effectively communicate with everyone you know when you just take the time to understand their motivations. I don't think I need to explain that similar personalities make for good relationships. A strong overbearing type will too easily manipulate or control a timid/ needy person; sometimes without them even realizing it. Pay attention and learn to identify the following:

The Strong Overbearing Type

This is the power person. You need dominance, winning, approval, accomplishments, validation, power, rewards, title and position. You love to dominate the conversation, talk about yourself, take credit, take risks, and be in charge. You can be arrogant and condescending to others.

You may sometimes pick an argument just to unload your opinions. You tend to be neat, confident, aggressive and in control. Your combative nature can make it very difficult for others to see past your authoritative exterior. You do care about others, but tend to make your own problems and needs your first priority.

The People Pleasers

This is the warm and smiling friend. You desire acceptance by family and peers, to always feel included, and to please everyone around you. You have sincere relationships and seek to keep the harmony in any situation.

You are cooperative, active in your community or workplace, and have a casual way about you. You often care about what others think and solicit opinions on a steady basis. You are usually smiling and happy and fun to be around. You don't like confrontation or drama in any aspect of your life. You are a sharp dresser, a sincere friend and a reliable source of caring. You tend to be taken advantage of because of your need to feel involved. Your constant giving can be stretched to the limits, just be careful you don't lose yourself or someone close to you along the way.

The Make it Happens

This is the pioneer. You are honest, sincere and have a positive self worth. You are receptive to new ideas and like to take risks. You are analytical, self assured and thrive on opportunity of all kinds. You are proudly open minded and also take the time to see where others are coming from. You love to see not only yourself grow and achieve but to help others grow as well.
You have a great creative freedom about you and have excellent self direction. You dream something and then just simply make it happen. You make it look easy to just make up your mind and achieve your goals. Take the time in your relationships to seek out true compatibility and *then* you can happily jump in with both feet.

The Timid/Needy Type

This is walking breathing reluctance. You are nervous and introverted, quiet but polite. You crave order and predictability and detest controversial issues. You are reluctant to change and you love to operate in a methodical manner. You rarely admit your mistakes and require assurances before you move forward with an idea. You avoid taking risks because you fear all consequences.
You constantly solicit other people's opinions to fill in the gaps of your own self worth. Your habitual use of picking the predictable source over the unknown can keep you from finding the things you really seek and want. Do not let fear, insecurities and the need for predictability keep you from taking a real chance on happiness with something or someone new.

After you have identified your own personality traits from the above, make a list of everyone you know and see if you can match them to their personalities. Are your parents equally matched or does one dominate the other? How about your boss?

Now, make a list of everyone you have dated or have been attracted to and see if the two of you have or *had* the correct potential to blend easily without a lot of hidden agendas, fears or power struggles.

How'd you do? Write down the top 5 matches from both lists and keep them close.

1. _____

2. _____

3. _____

4. _____

5. _____

The Gaps

Core values and common relatable interests can be shaped and affected by our generational influences. These influences such as our basic ideals, technological advances, preferences in music and entertainment or changes around us such as political, religious and sociological events can all motivate us to more easily accept or *not* accept the ones we love.

Boomers

The Boomer Generation, which is anyone born from 1946-1964; grew up during the era of the hippie, flower child, free lovin, bra burning America. Boomers were interested in initiating positive equal changes and wanted the world to notice. Many people who sprouted from this generation tend to be "all about me", and have an inwardly focused perception.

Boomers can be slightly more trusting and naïve about not only business opportunities and love relationships, but also about marriage. To them, work and status are usually a bigger priority than their family or intimate relationships. Many couples from this generation married fairly young and stayed in codependent relationships because they saw their own parents suffer through it. It is very evident in many of these relationships that one person rules the nest and the other follows. Boomers are unique, and love recognition. They have interestingly enough grown used to the status quo and are not as interested in change as they once were. Many individuals from this generation have waited in silence until their children were grown and then flew the coop for a more compatible mate.

GEN X

The Generation X'ers, which is anyone born from 1965-1979 have their own set of values too. Because their baby boomer parents were very career focused and women were just beginning to enter the workplace in droves, Generation X is now commonly known as the generation of "latch key" kids.

Most were the children of two working parents or divorce and practically raised themselves. People from this generation are more used to being alone or in small groups and prefer closely knit settings.

Generation X, unlike their parents are more insightful and focused on a work/life balance. Their careers are more of a means to support a lifestyle, but they do not let it define their life. Generation X highly values education as a means to not only provide for their family but to help feed the need this 80's generation has for knowledge and advancement.

They are the least trusting of the three generations mentioned here and are usually well informed before making any decisions. They are straight forward and focused but can be impatient with those who are either too materialistic or cynical. The 80's generation believes it can achieve all things. "I mean *like* we had Star Wars, Superman, ET, Michael Jackson and The Goonies as role models" Everything that was dreamt was within reach. A balanced career and love life is possible to this group who doesn't like to be told otherwise by different generational naysayers.

Generation Y

The Y Generation, which is anyone born from 1980-1997, is just as unique. Gen Y wants to take over the world without first learning how. Growing up in a world of instant gratification, these rookies don't remember what it was like to not have the availability of microwaves, cell phones or video games.

This group is very consumer driven and tend to rate their own self worth by what they can buy rather than waste time being overly insightful about themselves. Not usually good with finances at all, many life aspects for this generation are often chaotic, indecisive and needy. They need to buy the latest phone, purse, dress etc. and someone else needs to foot the bill. What? I can't continue living at home and I have to pay my own rent? They are experts at guilting a parent or relationship partner into fixing their life. This group belittles experience over youthful vigor, the poster child's for know it alls, even my own daughter's favorite saying is "I was telling ya"…

Easily bored, this generation craves continuous stimulation, information and activities to be happy; the funny thing is they actually have closer belief systems to their grandparent's non intimate relationships, than with the Generation Xers fundamental ideals. If you are a Generation Y, you need to find a mate with the same basic life desires as you or you will eventually get bored and move on.

Dating Gaps

Because we all change and grow over time it may be tempting for us to believe we can find a "mature" guy if we date someone much older than us, or a "fun" guy if we date someone much younger. These kinds of relationships can be fun for awhile but sooner or later the fundamental differences between you will creep their way into your "fun" and give you a harsh dose of reality. Instead of thinking you need to latch on to someone from another generation to fill a gap or a need in your life you may want to hold off until you uncover the real reasons you think you need them.

Example: If a 19 year old woman dates a 26 year old guy she may think she has got it made. He can show her the ropes and hopefully pay his and maybe even her own bills, what a catch right? But when she finally reaches 30 and he is approaching a mid life crisis, I guarantee you that things will change. He will tire of babysitting and either desire someone closer in age or have a string of flings to fill his boredom and bitterness. She will realize she wants someone else who is more compatible and will eventually leave him behind. Generation gap relationships can sometimes work. But if the two of you are "off" in other areas of compatibility such as finances or personality traits, you are asking for a lot of trouble at some point down the road.

CHAPTER 4 BASIC COMPATIBILITY TEST

1. When it comes to hiccups and crisis does your man step up to the plate or does he revert back to Neverland mode?

   Steps up to be a real man? 15 pts _____

   Peter Pan? 0 pts _____

   Does he fall somewhere in between? 5 pts _____

2. Does he answer his phone and offer assistance when you need him?

   Answer and Assist? 10 pts _____

   Pass the buck? Subtract 5 pts -_____

3. Has he alluded to having commitment issues when it comes to past relationships?

   No? 10 pts _____

   Yes? subtract 5 -_____

   4A. For Moms: If you have children, is he open, supportive and accepting that you are a package deal?

   Yes? 5 pts _____

   4B. For Non Parents: If you don't have children, has he shared any thoughts as to having a similar plan on children, child rearing or even having children someday at all that matches your future desires?

Yes? 5 pts _____

5. Are you both from the same generation, or at least less than 5 years apart?

Yes? 5 pts (Remember generation gaps can work but they can be more difficult) _____

   6. Do you share similar personalities or at least traits that you can tolerate daily?

Yes? 5 pts _____

0-25 pts
Hmm… Hope you like green tights Wendy, you are better off dating Hook, at least he owns a boat.

26-30 pts Careful Tink, He's a Borderline Lost Boy

31-50 pts Lucky, Lucky Girl

The key is to look for the person who has so much compatibility with you, it makes every date seem like an effortless match made in heaven, who knows, maybe it was…

Chapter 5
Commitment

Timing your Life

There is no such thing as perfect timing, simply because *perfect* in the human world does not exist. We can try our best to decide what is best for us and when, but sometimes the universe throws surprises our way for reasons that we do not understand.
I had a surprise like that. I dated a guy my senior year in high school for one month and then found out the following month I was expecting. Pregnant at 18.
I could have chosen abortion sure, but for reasons very personal to me I chose to keep my baby. The father and I were married a year later when our son was two and a half months old. Was it easy to raise a child at my age? No of course not. Was my fourteen year marriage a super fun cake walk? Obviously not or I wouldn't have written this book.

I am not here to promote teen pregnancy, or make it sound glamorous in any way; it is anything but a walk in the park, especially for young women who are alone. However, for me, even though it was a struggle at times, it was a decision I do not regret. Although money was sometimes an issue, love and patience were never missing from my parenting. Everyone has their own idea as to what is right and wrong in these situations, more specifically what is right for them. I could have ended the pregnancy and then waited like so many women today who choose to have their children in their 30's and 40's after they have achieved some level of success. That is an option that seems to be becoming more accepted and somewhat mainstream.

But *every* decision we make in life has a consequence *and* a gift. The consequences can be great, or very painful or maybe even just a lesson learned. The *gifts*, are little surprises that our decision has somehow given us a new chance or opportunity.

My gift, is that at 36 years old I have already had the chance to share eighteen wonderful years watching that baby turn into a handsome, intelligent, funny young man. And you know what? Eighteen extra years of having a child present in my fading lifetime feels a lot more like a gift from the universe than a mistake. Life is too short to wish for perfection. Sometimes the things we think will ruin our chances at happiness are the very things that teach us, help us grow and bring us more joy than we can ever imagine.

"When you wholeheartedly believe that you have the capacity to love another human being and put them first in your life, and they have chosen to do the same; you will know that it's time."

It all Depends...
Codependency vs. Interdependency

During the last 30-40 years a lot has been said about dysfunctional families and relationships. Psychologists have made a large fortune diagnosing and treating it, television pokes fun and even occasionally encourages it; so how does one know what is considered healthy and "normal?"
At the dirty root of so many dysfunctional relationships is the always popular co-dependency problem. Why is it such a prevalent problem?

Because people rush into or hang on to old relationships without first taking the time to find out who they really are and who it is they should hang on to. Because of this fly by night courtship technique many men and women end up with a person who is simply not their equal. The scariest part is most people don't even realize they are taking part or causing a co dependency problem because they don't know how to recognize their own behavior flaws. They may say things like "well this was how I was raised", "My parents think just like me and they have been married for fifty years." That may be true, but did the thousands of codependent relationships of our parents and grandparents generations stay together because they were so compatible or because they felt they had no choice? Do they treat each other as equals and friends or does one parent rule the nest?

Men in particular may seek out an intelligent but meek girl who is kind yet easily manipulated as a mate to share his life with. A girl who is lovely and sweet but will depend on him either emotionally or financially; or both. With this type of relationship dynamic he is able to subtly control her while still feeling like the hero, he wants the stability of his comfort zone and the hopeful desire that she will not have the fortitude to someday abandon him.

This personality will claim he is all for relationship equality, but his actions will speak otherwise. This is more like a parent child relationship than an adult partnership. Mr. Wrong will have passive aggressive tendencies and may even be physically or emotionally abusive. He more than likely won't even realize that his "plan" at this type of future with someone is wrong on so many levels or that it will almost certainly backfire in his face.

A codependent woman will feel she needs her partner in various aspects of her life. She will not openly admit that she wants a sugar daddy type husband who is her hero, but deep down her yearning for stability will push her to settle for Mr. "I guess he will do for right now." She may have been brought up rather poor, or used to a comfortable life where mommy and daddy provided her with everything. She relishes the good things in life and feels if he has a stable home environment where money is not an issue she can someday achieve her goals. Make no mistake; she knows deep down in her soul that this man that she cares for and is so emotionally and financially attached to is not her soul mate. But she stays long enough to convince herself that he must be "the one". Why?

She needs to stay long enough to experience the lovely wedding and sometimes a few children just in case it doesn't happen with someone else. Tick tock ya know…After some time has passed she then begins building a life of her own. It may be with friends, work, an affair or otherwise to fill the void she feels from her relationship. If she finds what she feels is her equal along the way, it's sayonara ville to husband number 1.

Note* If a man marries a woman who is too controlling like the situation in the first paragraph above, he will eventually find a way out as well.

So here they are, the happy couple, each thinking they have the American dream set up to last a lifetime. They get married, buy a house and forgivingly giggle when their partner forgets to put the sugar away. It is the best life ever for about 3-5 years and then true intention colors begin to shine a bit more brightly. Of course he was great when you were dating, why, because as Chris Rock says "you were just dating his representative."

In a codependent relationship it doesn't matter if you were dating for 7 short months or 7 long years. After you get married and "catch" each other the reality of the intentions behind your partnership will be unveiled. Now he is the guy you complain to your friends and co-workers about because he didn't pick up any diapers from the store, or tries to pick fights with you for no reason. What, your sweet codependent wife is nagging you? Hold up, that wasn't part of the plan, she was supposed to stay the same sweet but slightly needy girl I married forever. She promised she would never change or take me for granted.

The truth is painful ladies and gentlemen isn't it?

The truth is that they are both naïve, selfish and wrong; *and* about 80% of the reason that over half of the marriages in this country end in divorce. There are a few areas in life where codependency is acceptable and healthy, for example a toddler needing his mother or a crash victim needing some help from EMS.

However, educated couples need to realize that true compatibility is never a co-dependent situation; it is supposed be *interdependent*. It is not acceptable or realistic to expect a co dependent adult love relationship to have a happy ending. If you have tried to convince yourself otherwise, you are in denial and probably full of shit, so look in the mirror and ask yourself why you are in the relationship you are in? If you can still either lie to yourself, or tell me that you know at your very core that the man you share your life with is your equal, than you are in better shape than most. If not, then sure…try to stick it out forever and be the unhappy martyr in the relationship just to prove a point. Let me know how that's workin out for ya when you're sleeping in different bedrooms in twenty years.

What is built into our genetics and personality traits isn't going to change down the road because your controlling husband brought you flowers or your codependent girlfriend gets a job. Unless you have seen each other as equals from the very beginning, eventually one of you will leave or will probably be at the very least habitually unfaithful.

Pay attention from now on as to how you really treat your partner and to how and what your partner expects of you, it may save you a lifetime of trouble and the cost of a messy divorce.

The Big Fight

Even after months of seemingly Nirvanic bliss, an argument or disagreement between you and your partner is bound to happen sooner or later. Although you may share an almost perfect compatibility; personality quirks, mood swings and just plain old bad days can quickly spiral into a hurtful, no going back blaming contest if you are not careful.

We tend to always take things out on the ones we love, why? Because we know they care. Some of us confront and handle anger with shouting, stomping, name calling and slamming of doors. Others bottle up their anger for months until it finally blows up in their partner's face like a steamy water balloon of poo..

Depending on your personality and learned behavior, how you handle your partner's outbursts as well as your own can make or break your relationship when it comes to the inevitable fights that occur with our lovely mates.

However, violence against your partner is never ok. Physical or emotional abuse of any kind is not only unhealthy, it is downright dangerous. No excuse is good enough to hit someone you love. People try to legitimize domestic violence because they say the other person really deserved it, or it made them feel better to punish the spouse who may have hurt them emotionally.

The only thing that is *proven* or taught with domestic violence is that you are emotionally unstable, immature and unable to properly vent or express and communicate your anger in a healthy way. Period.

Honesty at all costs is vital during any disagreement, finding out you have been lied to after you are already angry at someone will lead to bitterness and distrust. Trust is a very fragile thing, so handle with care.

Be open often with your partner about your wants, needs, fears and desires in life. Don't plop them all down in each other's lap during a disagreement as sharply edged weapons or unhappy surprises.

If something is bothering you and you would discuss it with a close friend, your partner should be aware of your thoughts and fears too. Just because you have found someone you are compatible with now, doesn't mean you can read each other's minds.

-Now kiss and make up

Letting go

Breaking up is hard to do. If you honestly love someone for all of the right reasons, but come to the realization that you will not be receiving his love in return; it can feel like getting hit by a double decker bus. Depending on the situation, it may feel like a knife in your heart or sometimes in your back if he has chosen someone else over you.

Trying to hold on to someone who really isn't there is a mistake we have all made probably at least once. You must let him go…

Just because you have learned what makes couples relationships work doesn't mean he has. Maybe he is immature and wants to play the field a bit longer. Maybe he is stuck in his "plan". Whatever his reason, in his mind it makes perfect sense. The more you beg and plead or try to convince him to stay; the more clingy, needy, and "crazy", he will see you as. You must let him go…

More than likely at this stage in his life if he is not ready for the plunge with you, or you just do not meet his expectations of his planned ideal mate. He probably doesn't even seem to know what he wants from one week to another.

Let him go… Let him date and eventually marry "his plan" if that is his dream. At least you will have the solace that one day when his plan falls apart, he will remember what he could have had with you. In that moment he will be the one with bus tracks on his forehead and his heart.

The pain will fade over time, no need to drag it out into a flamboyant display of vengeful rebuttals or life unraveling conspiracy's. Save the drama for your mama.

Let him go…

If you are the one leaving, end it with all of the self respect, kindness, honorable intentions and self composure of a queen. Who knows maybe you two can eventually be friends.

Respecting yourself whether you are leaving a man or being left behind is the image that will haunt him forever.
Take heart in that, and say goodbye…

Commitment is a Choice

To be committed to a cause you truly believe in is to not waiver whatever hardships you may endure. Because people's thoughts and ideas have the tendency to ebb and flow over time as you grow older, just choosing to commit to a person is not enough. You must actually commit to the *cause* of you, the both of you.

When you love someone but they make you angry, or when you are committed to someone and they really let you down; just turning your back on them seems more easily justified.

But when you are committed to not only the other person but to the "cause" of your relationship, you realize that the natural ebb and flow, ups and downs, emotional outbursts and otherwise that your partner displays are in yourself as well.

If you have made it this far and your compatibility is obvious to both of you, don't throw it away because of a silly misunderstanding. Even the most compatible couples can use a silly fight as a reason to say forget it or wonder if it can work.

A person looking for an excuse to cheat, experiment or play around behind your back will often instigate an argument or take a silly misunderstanding way out of proportion as a way to lessen the guilt on themselves and blame you for what they are feeling. Another clue, cheaters often assume you are cheating too and will more than likely accuse you of some ridiculous desires that have never even crossed your mind. They may even state that their concocted assumption was just "the last straw" so they can feel freer to play the field for awhile.

It's not until you recognize the gift you have found in each other and choose to be committed to your cause that your walk together will have real meaning and have a chance at lasting for a lifetime.

Commitment is truly a choice that should not be taken lightly, it should not be as a result of a rebound relationship, family pressure or ever used as an ultimatum. Don't go bouncing back to your longtime ex who is your ex for a reason just to have a commitment of some kind in your life.

Unless you are both ready to make the choice whole heartedly to move forward together, one of you is going to be very disappointed in the end.

Don't let it be you...

What is love?

As we have explored together in previous chapters the physiological effects of our biological perception of the feeling otherwise known as love; we discovered that the "magic" we feel is actually a chemical reaction. You will remember that during the attachment phases of a relationship you will experience a type of euphoria which is triggered by the chemicals in our bodies and stimulate feelings of attachment and addiction.

This sensation is what they call "crazy in love." It is very similar to our body's reaction to chocolate and in fact a similar physiological effect occurs. These reactions/addictions usually last anywhere from three months to five years and then begin to fade. It has been evolutionarily designed for us to find a mate, procreate, raise and provide for a small child, and then move on to repeat the process.

I am sorry if this is a disappointment to anyone reading this book, but human beings are not programmed to be monogamous, monogamy is actually a learned behavior. Maybe even a forced behavior depending on your personal and religious beliefs. We choose to search for lifelong companionships and soul mates as humans because we abhor loneliness, we want to share our lives with others and give our existence meaning.

In order for you to be successful with all of the evolutionary odds stacked against you, it must be a joint venture, where both parties understand the risks and choose to walk forward into the unknown future anyway.

Because of the short lived design, true love and compatibility must be measured, explored, examined and tested over time. Unless the proper compatibility components are in place *before* embarking on a serious commitment; you may not only experience the famous 5-7 year itch, you may actually have a rash of disappointing relationships and break-ups.

So what then is "Love"?

Love is the compatibility that's still left when the euphoria fades away. When you still want to walk hand in hand as your hair grays, your figure slumps, and your medicine cabinet grows.
Love is the sincere enjoyment of each other's company because of shared interests, thoughts and beliefs. Love is caring for your partner's happiness more than just your own selfish wants and needs and they eagerly do the same for you.
Love isn't giving of yourself when it is easy and convenient for you. Love is giving of yourself when it is hard, and when it hurts like hell.

Love is *not* that crazy I can't live without you feeling, love is knowing that you can live without someone but you choose not to because you are just happier together. Love quite simply, is sharing your life with your best friend.

Chapter 5 Compatibility Test

1. Do you understand the differences between physiological "love" and real caring?

Yes =+10 pts. _____0 for no_____

2. Does he tell you what he is really thinking and feeling everyday or does he wait until you have an argument to unload his fears, insecurities and anger?

Throws the pent up anxiety in your face? Subtract 5 pts.- _____

3. Has your partner proven that they can handle real commitment without wavering or having a wandering eye?

Yes =+ 10 pts. _____0 for no

4. Can you let someone go when you realize you are not really equally compatible with them even if they don't, or your just not ready to let go?

Yes =+10 pts._____no subtract 10 pts.-_____

5. Has your partner ever been physically violent with you?

Yes= Subtract20 pts-_____And please get some help before *and* after you leave him.

20 -30 pts You have an excellent chance at having a solid commitment someday.

11-19 pts You and or your partner still have a lot of learning to do about love and commitment.

0-10 pts Your relationship and emotional boundaries are too unhealthy.

Negative points? _____ Dial 911

Final Intentions Exam

Hint: Add your positive numbers together first and then subtract the negatives for your final answer.

1. Do you have at least 3 basic ideals or activities in common?

Yes =+10 pts,_____o for no_____

2. Is there *now* anything about him you feel you want to change now or later?

(Yes = 1 pt. for honesty No = 4 pts for compatibility)_____

3. Does he have more than 5 characteristics of a sociopath?

Subtract 5 pts. for Yes -_____ 0 for no_____

4. Do you feel like you need to be in a relationship at all costs even if you are not that happy? Be honest…

Subtract 5 pts. for Yes -_____ + 5 for no_____

5. Do your spidey senses tingle when he is telling you where he was last night?

Yes Subtract 2 pts. -_____0 for no_____

6. Is his behavior often shady, flaky or unreliable?

Yes Subtract 5 pts. -_____0 for no_____

7. Has he exhibited any *lying* body language when being asked a direct question?

No = + 10 pts _____0 for yes_____

8. Does he seem to enjoy sharing control with you?

Yes = + 5 pts _____0 for no_____

9. Do the two of you have powerful sexual chemistry?

Yes = + 10 pts._____0 for no_____

10. Has he proven that he can be counted on during a crisis, or his he more worried about how your crisis will affect him?

He handles crisis well +10 pts ___ Turns a cold shoulder Subtract 10 pts.-___

11. Does he answer his phone and offer assistance when you need him?

Yes +5 pts. _____0 for no_____

12. Has he mentioned having commitment issues when it comes to past relationships?
Yes subtract 10 pts. - _____0 for no_____

13. Do you share the same astrological sign grouping?

Yes + 10 pts. _____0 for no_____

14. Are your personality traits compatible?

Good compatible traits + 10 pts. _____ 0 for no_____

15. Are you from the same generation?

Yes + 10 pts. _____0 for no_____

16. Historically has your significant other shown that their ideals about work, child rearing and finances/ saving $ are up to par with yours?

    No subtract 15 pts. -_____ (some of the biggest reasons for divorce)

17. Has he cheated on you even once?

    Yes: subtract 20 pts.- _____ He obviously did it for a reason, none of which are good. (Sadly the saying "once a cheater always a cheater is usually true.")

18. Do either one of you show signs of controlling or co-dependent behavior?

    Yes subtract 10 pts.- _____0 for yes

19. Do you simply have a lot of fun together without even trying?

    Yes: + 20 pts. _____0 for no_____

20. Does he wait until you argue to tell you about his insecurities & red flags?

    Yes: Subtract 5 pts. _____0 for no_____

21. Has he shown you through his actions that he truly cares for you?

Yes: + 10 pts ____Sometimes: + 5____No: Subtract 5.____

22. After reading this book, do you believe that the two of you have chosen to be in a committed relationship together because of all of the right, truly compatible, unselfish and non controlling or co-dependant reasons?

Be Honest:.....

Yes: +15 pts. _____0 for no_____

23. Do you now have a better understanding of what real love and commitment is?   Do you share that understanding with your partner?

Yes: +10 pts. _____0 for no_____

24. Do you know deep down in your very core that the person you are currently with is with you for all of the *right* compatible reasons?

No: Subtract 10 pts. -_____0 for yes_____

25. Are you still secretly silently looking for the person you really want, or hoping that your current partner just somehow or someday becomes that ideal?

Yes: Subtract 30 pts. -_____0 for no_____

26. Do you love your partner enough to really let them go and let them find the right person for them, or are you just holding on because you don't want to see them with someone else?
Be Honest...

Yes: I will let them go to find the real love they deserve= +25 pts. _____

No: I will just try and make it work, I think we will be ok. Subtract 30 pts.-___

27. Would *they* realize "trying" just isn't real love and let you go?

Be Honest...

Yes: + 40 pts. _____ There is no greater love.

No: They would probably keep me around while they are shopping for someone else overtime.. Subtract 40 pts. -_____

Add Positive Score_____

Subtract Negative Score_-_____

Your Total Score_____

Negative points?
Please don't get too discouraged, just move on as quickly as you can.

0- 49 pts.
I think you know the right thing to do. Don't give up on finding true love or just hold onto something you know deep down isn't the real thing. Don't be the person who decides not to heed the compatibility warning signs because you think that somehow you two are just gonna magically be different then everyone else's failed relationships. Even if you both decided it will work, something crucial is missing here. It doesn't matter how long you have been together. Sooner or later if you stay in this relationship someone is going to be hurt. Don't let it be you.

50-99 pts.
This is a hard place to be, although this compatibility is not a lost cause, real compatibility either just simply exists or it just doesn't. You may be better off as lifelong pals if you ever feel like you have had to "try" and make things work. If that is the case, one of you is

bound to start "shopping" behind the other's back eventually. One or both of you are in this relationship for the wrong reasons. It is better to find out who it is now before you waste anymore time. I think if you sit down and reflect on what you have read and honestly apply it towards your relationship, you will have the answer.

100-174 pts.
-----Congratulations, I am so proud and happy for you for finding a truly compatible partner. Although no relationship is ever perfect or always happy, you have enough shared basic compatibility traits to see each other through the hard times and life's daily struggles. If you have both decided on a commitment for all of the right reasons, your ending has every chance at being very happy. I hope for your sake your partner has also taken enough time to realize what true love and compatibility is, or one day he will wish that he had; and he will remember what he has lost in you. Make it a point to communicate openly with each other and you will have a great chance at a happy, successful, lifelong relationship.

Closing

What a personal rollercoaster writing this book has been for me. It has allowed me to step out of my school girl box of naivety and look at the big picture. I had reached a point where I had to rip my own heart out, reassemble the pieces in a better way and stuff them back in.

It is interesting that we as women have learned to expect something from men and ourselves, that in many aspects is so very unrealistic. It is not until we learn to create a stronger sense of self and demand honest relationships that we will be truly ready to handle the honesty that comes along with it. If we want equality we must stop enabling men and demand it.

We have created in our collective power puff minds an invented prince that thinks 80% with his heart and mind, and 20% with his penis, but because of genetics and testosterone alone it is really closer to the other way around. A recent study uncovered that a woman feels her most vulnerable human part is her heart, a man, his testicles…enough said.

Trying to ask them to change their testosterone driven genetics is just as silly as them asking us to stop awing at snuggly kitty cats and babies. The middle ground of understanding is where the magic happens. Real compatibility comes when you can be honest with each other about your wants needs and desires, throw preconceived notions about romantic relationships to the wind and accept each other as perfectly normal, flawed as hell, but equally compatible individuals. When you can do that, and look into each other's eyes, the connection will knock you off your feet.

Do not be limited in your dreams or efforts by the mistakes others have made before you, you are limitless potential until your last breath. Each of us deserves to walk through this life with our head held high, a smile on our face, love in our hearts, and a partner in our hand. It is my sincere hope for you that you will find him.

A Hope Endured

A quiet thought, and thoughtful glance may all be thrown to circumstance, but a hope endured will always pay the greater dividend some day.

A step into the darkest night, becomes a whirling deafened fight, but a walk in love will surely bring, a time to dance a song to sing.

The metamorphosis of my broken soul, embraced my mind and made silent tears cry, my past crumples around me, as I awaken, to peek outside and learn to fly...

Angela DeVere

For the Boys

It is not by coercion or trickery that heartfelt change is ever truly accomplished, but by hearing, understanding and acknowledging the need for changes within your own heart."

-AD